C000143365

Advanced Introduction to International

Elgar Advanced Introductions are stimulating and thoughtful introductions to major fields in the social sciences and law, expertly written by the world's leading scholars. Designed to be accessible yet rigorous, they offer concise and lucid surveys of the substantive and policy issues associated with discrete subject areas.

The aims of the series are two-fold: to pinpoint essential principles of a particular field, and to offer insights that stimulate critical thinking. By distilling the vast and often technical corpus of information on the subject into a concise and meaningful form, the books serve as accessible introductions for undergraduate and graduate students coming to the subject for the first time. Importantly, they also develop well-informed, nuanced critiques of the field that will challenge and extend the understanding of advanced students, scholars and policy-makers.

Titles in the series include:

International Political Economy
Benjamin J. Cohen

The Austrian School of Economics
Randall G. Holcombe

Cultural Economics
Ruth Towse

Law and Development
Michael J. Trebilcock and Mariana Mota Prado

International Humanitarian Law
Robert Kolb

International Tax Law
Reuven S. Avi-Yonah

Post Keynesian Economics
J.E. King

International Intellectual Property
Susy Frankel and Daniel J. Gervais

International Conflict and Security Law
Nigel D. White

Comparative Constitutional Law
Mark Tushnet

International Human Rights Law
Dinah L. Shelton

Entrepreneurship
Robert D. Hisrich

International Trade Law
Michael J. Trebilcock

Public Policy
B. Guy Peters

The Law of International Organizations
Jan Klabbers

International Environmental Law
Ellen Hey

Advanced Introduction to

International Environmental Law

ELLEN HEY

Erasmus School of Law, Erasmus University Rotterdam, the Netherlands

Elgar Advanced Introductions

Edward Elgar
PUBLISHING

Cheltenham, UK • Northampton, MA, USA

Published by
Edward Elgar Publishing Limited
The Lypiatts
15 Lansdown Road
Cheltenham
Glos GL50 2JA
UK

Edward Elgar Publishing, Inc.
William Pratt House
9 Dewey Court
Northampton
Massachusetts 01060
USA

A catalogue record for this book
is available from the British Library

Library of Congress Control Number: 2015950301

ISBN 978 1 78195 456 0 (cased)
ISBN 978 1 78195 457 7 (paperback)
ISBN 978 1 78195 458 4 (eBook)

Typeset by Servis Filmsetting Ltd, Stockport, Cheshire
Printed on FSC approved paper
Printed and bound in Great Britain by Marston Book Services Ltd, Oxfordshire

Contents

Preface

The book in your hands has the character of a long essay that attempts to illustrate and assess where international environmental law stands at the beginning of the twenty-first century. It focuses on themes that play a role in international environmental law discourse, instead of providing a systematic overview of international environmental regimes.

The text is indebted to the work of many of my colleagues who research and write in the area of international environmental law, even if this is not reflected in the text because it lacks references to their work. I thank my colleagues who work in the area of international environmental law for their many valuable publications and much cherished opportunities for discussion. I am particularly indebted to Jutta Brunnée, Jonas Ebbesson and Louis Kotzé who generously gave me their time by reading through the whole draft manuscript and offering their thoughts on how it could be improved. Alessandra Arcuri equally generously gave me her time and thoughts with regard to the parts of the text related to the relationship between international environmental law and international trade and investment law. Thanks a million Jutta, Jonas, Louis and Alessandra. Needless to say the usual disclaimer applies.

The exclusion of references from the text is related to the publisher's request to limit them. I have perhaps taken this request to the extreme by including references only to what I consider to be important texts, by non-lawyers or bodies, that have influenced how we think about the protection and conservation of the environment. The choice was also made to omit full references to relevant instruments and cases in the text. Instead, information about relevant instruments is found in the table of instruments, while documents that are more difficult to find, such as resolutions of international bodies, are parenthesized in the text. Moreover, acronyms for treaty instruments are included in the table of instruments, not the table of abbreviations. Full references to case citations are included in the table of cases.

I thank the Erasmus School of Law, of Erasmus University Rotterdam, for enabling me to take a number of sabbaticals and the Faculty of Law, of the University of New South Wales, for accommodating me during these sabbaticals. It was during two of these sabbaticals that most parts of this text were written.

Finally, Ben Booth, of Edward Elgar, thank you for your never ending tolerance regarding the ever forward moving deadline and for your encouragement throughout.

Abbreviations

ACCC	Aarhus Convention Compliance Committee
ACHPR	African Commission on Human and People's Rights
ASEAN	Association of Southeast Asian Nations
BAT	best available technology
BEP	best environmental practices
BIT	bilateral investment treaty
CAO	Compliance Advisor/Ombudsman
CBNRM	community-based natural resource management
CDM	Clean Development Mechanism
CERs	certified emission reductions
CFCs	chlorofluorocarbons
CMP	conference of the parties acting as the meeting of the parties
CO_2	carbon dioxide
COP	conference of the parties
CSD	Commission on Sustainable Development
DRC	Democratic Republic of Congo
EAF	Ecosystem Approach to Fisheries
EBRD	European Bank for Reconstruction and Development
ECOSOC	Economic and Social Council of the United Nations
ECtHR	European Court of Human Rights
EEZ	exclusive economic zone
EIA	environmental impact assessment
FAO	Food and Agriculture Organization of the United Nations
FIT	feed-in-tariff
FSC	Forest Stewardship Council
GEF	Global Environment Facility
GESAMP	Joint Group of Experts on the Scientific Aspects of Marine Environmental Protection
GHG	greenhouse gas
IAComHR	Inter-American Commission on Human Rights
IACtHR	Inter-American Court of Human Rights

IADB	Inter-American Development Bank
IAEA	International Atomic Energy Agency
IBRD	International Bank for Reconstruction and Development
ICJ	International Court of Justice
ICSID	International Centre for the Settlement of Investment Disputes
IDA	International Development Agency
IDBs	international development banks
IFC	International Finance Corporation
ILA	International Law Association
ILC	International Law Commission
ILO	International Labour Organization
IMO	International Maritime Organization
INDCs	intended nationally determined contributions
IPCC	Inter-governmental Panel on Climate Change
IPT	international peoples' tribunal
ISF	International Shipping Federation
ISO	International Organization for Standardization
ITLOS	International Tribunal for the Law of the Sea
IUCN	International Union for Conservation of Nature
IUPN	International Union for the Protection of Nature
IWC	International Whaling Commission
KAZA	Kavango Zambezi Transfrontier Conservation Area
LMOs	living modified organisms
MA	Millennium Ecosystem Assessment
MDGs	Millennium Development Goals
MEA	multilateral environmental agreement
MIGA	Multilateral Investment Guarantee Agency
MOP	meeting of the parties
MOU	memorandum of understanding
MPAs	marine protected areas
MRV	measurement, reporting and verification
MSC	Marine Stewardship Council
MSY	maximum sustainable yield
NGO	non-governmental organization
NIEO	New International Economic Order
OECD	Organisation for Economic Cooperation and Development
OP&Ps	Operational Policies and Procedures
PCA	Permanent Court of Arbitration
PCF	Prototype Carbon Fund
POPs	persistent organic pollutants

PVC	polyvinyl chloride
RFMO	regional fisheries management organization
Rio+20	Conference on Sustainable Development
SADC	Southern African Development Community
SDGs	Sustainable Development Goals
SEA	strategic environmental assessment
UNCED	United Nations Conference on Environment and Development/Rio Conference
UNCHE	United Nations Conference on the Human Environment/Stockholm Conference
UNDP	United Nations Development Programme
UNECE	United Nations Economic Commission for Europe
UNEP	United Nations Environment Programme
UNESCO	United Nations Educational, Scientific and Cultural Organization
UNGA	United Nations General Assembly
UNIDO	United Nations Industrial Development Organization
USSR	Union of Soviet Socialist Republics
WBIP	World Bank Inspection Panel
WCED	World Commission on Environment and Development
WMO	World Meteorological Organization
WTO	World Trade Organization
WWF	World Wide Fund for Nature

1   Setting the scene

1.1 Introduction

This chapter sets the scene and its first section provides a rough sketch of the types of problems that contemporary international environmental law seeks to address and of the complex institutions that constitute it. Accordingly, this first section considers three questions: what does international environmental law deal with, who makes it and where do we find it? The remainder of the chapter considers issues of terminology, and sets out the aims and outline of the book.

1.2 The what, who and where of contemporary international environmental law

1.2.1 What does international environmental law deal with?

International environmental law aims to address the negative impacts that humans have on the environment with the objective of protecting and conserving the environment. Human impacts on the environment derive from the myriad of activities that we engage in, including the introduction of substances into the environment and the taking of elements from the environment for direct human use or for developing products that are useful to humans. Think of, respectively, the introduction of chemicals into the environment through the use of pesticides in agriculture or as a result of hydraulic fracturing (fracking) in the process of mining shale gas; the taking of fish or other wild animals for human consumption or as hunting trophies; and the use of timber as building material or minerals in industrial processes.

Human life depends on natural processes such as the pollination of plants by insects, the purification of water by wetlands and the protective shield that the ozone layer provides against an overdose of ultraviolet sunlight. While some of the benefits that nature offers can be provided by technological developments, relevant technologies may not be affordable everywhere and may themselves give rise to new environmental problems. Waste water treatment technology provides an example. While primary treatment – to remove solids and grease by way of mechanical treatment – is relatively affordable, secondary treatment – to remove in particular organic material by way of microbial activity – and especially tertiary treatment – to remove among other things chemicals and nutrients by way of a variety of processes – are more expensive. Moreover, each of these phases of waste water treatment results in residues which need to be made fit for reuse or safely disposed of.

In addition to the human uses referred to above, humans also value the environment for its role in cultural and spiritual experiences. Think of, for example, the role nature plays in literature, movies and paintings as well as in our experience of the outdoors and the use of water in religious ceremonies. These experiences may prompt reflection on geological time and the fact that humans have only been around for a fraction of that time, even if human behaviour is impacting the Earth's systems, such as the climate system. Such ponderings may lead to the conclusion that the Earth's systems are worthy of protection in their own right. While thoughts of this nature may be on the minds of many who engage in the development and implementation of international environmental law, they find little explicit reflection in international environmental law. On the contrary, international environmental law reflects an anthropocentric approach to the protection and preservation of the environment, rather than an eco-centric approach. In other words, emphasis is on instrumental and human centric reasons for protecting and conserving the environment.

Perhaps the most striking element of contemporary international law is its focus on global interdependencies. This process has been fostered by our increased understanding of the Earth's systems, such as the climatic and oceanic systems, pointing to complex linkages within and among these systems and the linkages between these systems and human activities. A pertinent example of a set of interdependencies that international environmental law seeks to address is the following: greenhouse gas (GHG) emissions, resulting from a host of human activities, cause climate change which in turn causes sea level rise, excessive rain and flooding in some regions and extreme drought in other areas. The fact that our economic system spans the globe and creates interdependencies also has contributed to the emergence of international environmental law. Think of the fact that tropical rainforests provide inputs for medicinal products appreciated across the globe, resulting in calls to protect these forests. Economic incentives, moreover, foster global trade in, for example, oil and coal, agricultural products, chemicals, waste and genetically modified organisms. The generation, transportation and use of these products may harm the environment. In addition, due to contemporary communication facilities individuals and groups across the globe are ever more interconnected and engaged with each other, leading to transnational movements of, for example, indigenous peoples or environmental groups. These groups, aware of global interdependencies, demand that their concerns be addressed by international environmental law. Global interdependencies thus point to the complex linkages between natural systems, between social systems and among social and natural systems.

Despite these global interdependencies a considerable amount of contemporary international environmental law is concerned with bilateral relationships or with issues that involve relatively smaller groups of states. Pertinent examples are treaties that deal with international rivers or transboundary nature conservation areas. In addition, it is important to realize that the consequences of environmental harm manifest themselves at the most local of levels. Think of the farmer who experiences drought, the population of small island states who may see their island flooded, or the members of a local community who due to irresponsible logging or dumping of hazardous wastes see their livelihood and sometimes lives endangered. Moreover, action to address environmental problems ultimately depends on the decisions of individuals and groups in local situations.

1.2.2 Who makes international environmental law?

International environmental law is not only developed and implemented by states, but also by international organizations, individuals and groups in society as well as the non-governmental organizations (NGOs) and private sector actors. Treaties, or agreements between states, and international customary law, are prominent sources of international environmental law, yet their content may be co-determined by non-state actors. In addition, principles, standards and rules also emanate from international organizations, private sector actors, NGOs, sub-state actors and cooperative initiatives involving these actors as well as states. Non-state actors, moreover, engage in the application of these principles, standards and rules in specific situations and thereby may affect a variety of actors, including states. International environmental law thus involves a wide diversity of actors.

1.2.3   Where do we find international environmental law?

As the previous section implies international environmental law is found in instruments emanating from states as well as from non-state actors. It includes treaties and decisions of international organizations, private sector actors and NGOs. Relevant examples include multilateral environmental agreements (MEAs), decisions of conferences of the parties (COP) to MEAs, but also the Operational Policies and Procedures (OP&Ps) adopted by the World Bank[1] and the standards on the certification of sustainable forestry projects adopted by the Forest Stewardship Council (FSC), a multi-stakeholder organization. International environmental law also includes customary international law, such as the no harm principle (section 4.5.1) and arguably the precautionary principle (section 4.6.2).

Moreover, international environmental law is found not only in instruments that address classical environmental topics such as nature protection or the prevention of pollution. International watercourse law and international marine fisheries law, for example, also address topics that are relevant to the protection and conservation of the environment. Moreover, international environmental law is linked to other areas of international law such as human rights law, the law of armed conflict, international trade law and international investment law. International environmental law is also part of general international law. This entails that general international law, such as the law on treaties and the law that regulates state sovereignty and jurisdiction on land, at sea, in the air and in outer space, applies when environmental problems are addressed. It also means that discussions regarding, for example, the fragmented nature of international law or global governance are part of international environmental law discourse.

Finally, international environmental law is also intimately linked to national law. National law, national environmental law in particular, provides an important, even if not the only, means by way of which international environmental law is implemented and enforced.

---

1 The term World Bank refers to the International Bank for Reconstruction and Development (IBRD) and the International Development Agency (IDA).

1.3   Terminology

The title of this book uses the term *international* environmental law, which could be taken to imply that the book focuses solely on classical inter-state law. That would be a misconception since the days are long gone, if they ever existed (section 2.2.2), when international environmental law was the product of state interaction only. Instead this book, as explained in the previous section, includes the development of principles, standards and rules and their application by a variety of actors that in turn address the activities of a diversity of actors (section 2.5). Such an understanding of law includes what is referred to as *global* law and *transnational* law. The term "global law" refers to law that is not confined to a particular territory or territories and that aims to apply universally to all actors in similar situations. A relevant example is the principle of equitable and reasonable use as developed in international watercourse law (section 4.5.2). The term "transnational law" refers to law that concerns issues that are relevant across state boundaries, possibly globally, and that are addressed by a variety of actors. Relevant examples are cooperation between sub-state actors and NGOs with respect to the conservation and protection of the Rode Beek/Rodebach, a stream that flows across the border between Germany and the Netherlands (section 2.5), and the FSC, applying its certification standards to associated companies all over the world (sections 2.5, 6.4.3). While the former is an example of cross-border cooperation, the latter operates globally. Whether the latter is considered to be part of global law depends on one's definition of the term, in particular whether it includes norms developed by non-state actors and norms that do not apply universally because not all stakeholders have joined the regime, but do have global reach.

Two terms used throughout this book merit clarification: "normative development" and "executive decision-making". The term "normative development" refers to the adoption of principles, standards and rules of general application that aim to regulate the behaviour of states and other actors. Normative development is reflected in the instruments referred to in the previous section, including MEAs, COP decisions, the World Bank's OP&Ps and the FSC's certification standards. The term "executive decision-making" refers to a decision or act by which principles, rules or standards are applied to a specific situation. Relevant examples include the secretariat of the 1992 United Nations Framework Convention on Climate Change (UNFCCC) and its 1997 Kyoto Protocol, which under the authority of Executive Board of the Clean Development Mechanism (CDM), approves and registers certified emission reductions (CERs) from GHG reduction projects invested in by developed states but executed in developing states; the World Bank applying its OP&P on indigenous peoples to the design and execution of projects to protect biodiversity in a given state; and the FSC applying its certification standards to a timber producing company or to timber products.

Many of the instruments referred to above are regularly referred to as "soft law". The term soft law, however, may mean different things to different people and often serves as "a catch-all" phrase in which a wide variety of documents are encompassed that share a single trait: they are not legally binding according to classical international legal doctrine. Otherwise the documents vary considerably in terms of normative impact. For example, a draft treaty developed by an NGO cannot be equated with a decision of the COP of the climate change regime on how to account for CERs from CDM projects, even though both are not legally binding. The draft treaty may or may not have lasting normative impact depending on a myriad of factors, while the COP decision will govern projects that "count" in terms of the climate change regime. Due to the fact that it encapsulates so many different emanations of normative development, the term "soft law" will not be used in the remainder of this book.

1.4   Aims and outline

This book aims to provide insight into international environmental law by treating salient and at times controversial themes that arise in this area of law. Its objective is to foster awareness about why achieving the protection of the environment by way of international environmental law is often controversial and why international environmental law itself may give rise to controversy, for example in the North–South context (section 2.4). Relevant international environmental regimes, such as nature conservation treaties or the UNFCCC and its Kyoto Protocol, or salient moments in the development of international environmental law, such as the 1972 United Nations Conference on the Human Environment (UNCHE or Stockholm Conference), will be used as examples to illustrate particular points or developments. This book, then, does not provide a systematic overview of the various regimes that constitute international environmental law; such overviews are available in excellent (text)books on the subject.

The following themes are the subject of subsequent chapters: origins and development; evolving perceptions of what is at stake; principles; institutional structures; dispute settlement and accountability mechanisms; and the relationship with other areas of international law. The final chapter by way of conclusions considers the theme of continuity and change in international environmental law and identifies some of the challenges that international environmental law faces.

2 Origins and development

2.1 Introduction

In the development of international environmental law successive instruments and summits rarely break with the past; instead they build upon existing instruments and regulatory approaches, adding new instruments and regulatory approaches. Elements of international environmental law introduced in the early and mid-twentieth century thus continue to be relevant today, with new elements being added. This chapter emphasizes these continuities and additions and also traces the political history of international environmental law. It treats the following themes: early beginnings and continuity; from transboundary to global concerns; North–South relations; and the influence of actors other than states.

2.2 Early beginnings: continuity and change

During the late nineteenth and early twentieth centuries, the elite in Europe and North America established national nature conservation organizations which lobbied for the conclusion of treaties and the establishment of an international body that would promote nature conservation. Some, like the Dutchman Pieter Gerbrand van Tienhoven, argued that the international body should not be state-based but run by prominent persons, because states work slowly and their involvement can lead to complications. While the latter part of this statement may be true, international nature conservation law and international environmental law more generally attribute important roles to states.

2.2.1 Nature conservation treaties

Early efforts to put nature conservation on the international agenda resulted in the adoption of treaties that sought to conserve wild animals in colonial Africa. Relevant instruments are the 1900 Convention, the 1902 Convention and the 1933 Convention. They focused in particular on the conservation of those species that were in demand in the North for their feathers, songs or as wild game. Ironic is the fact that while demand in the North was at the source of the nature conservation problems in Africa, local populations were also barred from taking the protected species. As a result, the livelihoods of these local populations were negatively impacted. This problem may also manifest itself today when protected areas are instituted and the resources made available for compensating local populations and developing alternative livelihoods are scarce.

The 1900 and 1902 Conventions focused on the protection of useful species, not habitats, with the 1900 Convention also listing "harmful" species, such as lions and poisonous snakes, whose numbers were to be reduced. The 1933 Convention introduced protected areas, including national parks, as a measure to protect species, in conjunction with listed species, game laws and restrictions on trade in hunting trophies. The latter is an early example of the use of a trade measure in international environmental law.

A reoccurring controversy that goes back to the negotiation of the 1933 Convention, concerns the appropriateness of closed areas as a measure to protect species. Today it manifests itself in negotiations related to the establishment of marine protected areas (MPAs) in high seas areas. MPAs in high seas areas are controversial because they restrict the freedom of fishing, which continues to apply on the high seas despite its negative effect on the state of marine fish stocks, many of which are seriously overfished (section 5.2.3).

Relatively early in the development of international environmental law a nature conservation convention was also adopted for the Americas: the 1940 Western Hemisphere Convention. Like the 1933 Convention, it fostered the establishment of protected areas, including national parks, in order to protect endangered species. The Western Hemisphere Convention continues to be relevant for nature protection in the Americas today, although for Central America the 1992 Biodiversity and Wilderness Conservation Convention is now more important.

The main elements of the early nature conservation conventions still form the core of contemporary international nature protection law: species protection, protected areas, regulation of use and trade restrictions. The following are examples of contemporary conventions that use these measures, even if combining them with new ones. The 1996 African–Eurasian Waterbirds Agreement, concluded under the auspices of the 1979 Bonn Convention, and the 1973 Polar Bear Agreement protect species. The 1971 Ramsar Convention and the 1972 World Heritage Convention protect areas, respectively wetlands and natural heritage sites. The 1973 Convention on International Trade in Endangered Species of Wild Fauna and Flora (CITES) protects endangered species of flora and fauna by regulating or prohibiting their trade. Many of these conventions use the listing of species as means of prohibiting or regulating their taking or trade. For example, CITES, in its three appendices, lists species threatened with extinction that can only be traded in exceptional circumstances, such as for purposes of scientific research; species that require protection for their survival and whose trade is controlled; and species that are protected in at least one state and where this state has asked other CITES parties for assistance in controlling trade.

The 1992 Biodiversity Convention provides a broad framework for the protection of biodiversity and regulating its use. It and subsequent decisions taken under its auspices include elements of nature conservation law discussed above. Its preference for in situ conservation, for example, requires the establishment of protected areas, even if now combined with ecosystem-based governance approaches (Art. 8) (section 3.6.2). The Biodiversity Convention has also led to the institutionalization of cooperation with other international forums focused on nature protection, such as CITES. These forums are linked to each other by way of memoranda of understanding and joint work programmes. The Biodiversity Convention also introduced a new substantive dimension to nature conservation law – the protection of genetic resources – and added a new regulatory dimension – ex situ conservation. Genetic resources are defined as "genetic material of actual or potential value" (Art. 2) and the Biodiversity Convention aims to ensure both access to and fair and equitable sharing of benefits from their utilization (Art. 15), a topic that is further regulated in the 2010 Nagoya Protocol (section 4.5.6). While ex situ conservation is a well-known means of conservation in the form of seed banks, botanical gardens and zoos, its introduction into international nature conservation law was new at the time. The Biodiversity Convention regards ex situ conservation as complementary to in situ conservation (Art. 9).

2.2.2   Non-governmental organizations

NGOs have engaged with international environmental law since the early twentieth century. In 1913 the efforts of nature conservation organizations in Europe and North America resulted in the adoption of a treaty that sought to establish the *Commission Consultative pour la Protection Internationale de la Nature (Commission Consultative)*. Due to the advent of World War I, this body never convened. While the *Commission Consultative* was not revived after World War I, the predecessors of the International Union for Conservation of Nature (IUCN) were established, respectively, after World War I and World War II. The *Office International de Documentation et Corrélation pour la Protection de la Nature* was established in 1928 and the International Union for the Protection of Nature (IUPN) in 1948. In 1956 these institutions merged to form IUCN. IUCN, as IUPN, is a hybrid organization in that its members include national and international NGOs, ministries, such as the Ministry of Environment, Wildlife and Tourism of Botswana, and government agencies, such as the United States Environmental Protection Agency. IUCN's work is carried out by its employed staff and a large network of experts who contribute on a voluntary basis. In 1960, IUCN established the World Commission on Environmental Law and in 1970 the Environmental Law Center, in Bonn, Germany. Both institutions have been influential in the development of international environmental instruments, such as the 1982 World Charter for Nature (section 4.2) and the Biodiversity Convention.

Since the early twentieth century many NGOs have been established that focus on international environmental issues; their mandates may be issue-specific or of a more general nature. Examples of the former are Wetlands International and the Coalition for Access to Justice for the Environment. NGOs with a more general mandate include organizations such as IUCN, the World Wide Fund for Nature (WWF) and Greenpeace. All these organizations aim to influence the development of international environmental law through their active participation in international forums as observers and some, like Greenpeace, combine these activities with more action-oriented approaches. National, local and grassroots NGOs also influence the development of international environmental law. They do so, for example, when they access grievance mechanisms established by international actors, such as international development banks (IDBs) or NGOs (sections 6.4.1, 6.4.3), or when they access the compliance mechanisms established by the 1998 Aarhus Convention on transparency, public participation and access to justice in environmental matters (section 6.4.2), adopted within the framework of the United Nations Economic Commission for Europe (UNECE). Local and grassroots NGOs also act together at the international level to influence the development of international environmental law. They do so, for example, as observers at or via side-events organized in conjunction with international negotiating conferences, such as a COP. An example is the Global Forest Coalition. It was established by NGOs and indigenous peoples' organizations and seeks to influence both national and international policies related to forests. Private sector organizations, such as the International Shipping Federation (ISF), and organizations composed of NGOs and private sector organizations, such as the FSC, also influence the development of international environmental law (sections 2.5, 6.4.3).

Finally, international networks of experts, such as international environmental lawyers, also influence the development of international environmental law. These networks, also known as epistemic communities, are characterized by their informal institutional structure, with their participants typically meeting at international academic conferences and seminars. However, participants in epistemic communities also engage with states, NGOs, international organizations and the private sector as advisors or in more formal capacities. IUCN's World Commission on Environmental Law provides an example of how members of the epistemic community of environmental lawyers engage with an NGO and in fact form part of that NGO; membership of the Aarhus Convention's compliance committee provides an example of how members of the network of international environmental lawyers may engage with an international organization, the UNECE, and the states parties to the Aarhus Convention.

2.3   From transboundary to global concerns

During the late nineteenth and early twentieth centuries transboundary environmental issues also became a matter of concern. Early instruments focused on resource utilization and typically involved a relatively small number of states. Examples of treaties adopted in this period are the 1885 Treaty on Salmon Fishing in the Rhine concluded between Germany, the Netherlands and Switzerland; the 1909 Boundary Waters Treaty concluded between the United Kingdom (for Canada) and the United States; and the 1911 Fur Seals Convention concluded between Japan, Russia, the United Kingdom and the United States for the preservation of fur seals in the North Pacific Ocean. Some early regimes, such as the Boundary Waters Treaty, have accommodated contemporary environmental concerns and continue to be relevant today. The Boundary Waters Treaty is the basis for, among other agreements, the 1972 Great Lakes Agreement. The Great Lakes Agreement has been amended and renewed regularly, lastly in 2012. In its current form it is an example of a contemporary transboundary watercourse agreement, which promotes integrated water resources and ecosystem-based management (sections 3.6, 5.2.1).

Three famous arbitrations find their origin in these early transboundary concerns: the 1893 *Pacific or Bering Sea Fur Seal* arbitration between the United States and the United Kingdom concerning the exploitation of fur seals straddling United States' waters and areas beyond national jurisdiction; the 1941 *Trail Smelter* arbitration between the United States and Canada concerning transboundary air pollution; and the 1957 *Lac Lanoux* arbitration between Spain and France concerning a shared lake. While all three decisions emphasize the need for cooperation among the states concerned (section 4.4), the 1941 *Trail Smelter* award resounds most clearly in contemporary international environmental law. It is credited with the first formulation of the no harm principle (section 4.5.1). The tribunal held that:

> under principles of international law ... no State has the right to use or permit the use of its territory in such a manner as to cause injury by fumes on or in the territory of another or the properties therein, if the case is of serious consequence and the injury is established by clear and convincing evidence. (p. 1965)

Transboundary concerns continue to play a significant role in international environmental law. They form an important reason for concluding agreements related to international watercourses (rivers and lakes), regional seas, transboundary marine fish stocks and specific environments such as the Alps or transboundary conservation areas. An example of the latter is the Kavango Zambezi Transfrontier Conservation Area (KAZA), a cooperative project between Angola, Botswana, Namibia, Zambia and Zimbabwe, which is supported by a number of donor states and NGOs, including WWF (section 2.5).

During the 1960s and 1970s several publications that predicted environmental catastrophe if business-as-usual persisted, fuelled the development of contemporary (international) environmental law and emphasized linkages between humans and their environment across the globe.[1] The realization thus emerged that environmental problems may not be of only local, national, transboundary or regional significance but of universal, or global, concern. It led to the organization of world summits under the auspices of the United Nations. These summits in turn stimulated the adoption of MEAs and normative development more generally.

An early example of an MEA, one that predates the summits discussed below, is the 1954 Convention for the Prevention of Pollution of the Sea by Oil (OILPOL Convention). The term MEAs is used to refer to regional or global agreements that focus on environmental problems that are of global concern, such as the conservation of marine fish stocks or biological diversity and the reduction of climate change or pollution of the marine environment. Many MEAs are open to all states and have global coverage; others have regional coverage or membership. Examples of the former are the UNFCCC and the Biodiversity Convention. Examples of the latter are the 1979 UNECE Convention on Long-range Transboundary Air Pollution (LRTAP Convention), the 1991 Antarctic Environmental Protocol and the 1968 African Nature Conservation Convention, which replaced the 1933 Convention and will itself be replaced by the 2003 Revised African Nature Conservation Convention, when it enters into force. MEAs establish complex institutional structures (sections 5.2 and 5.3) and their work is closely linked to that of international organizations such as the World Bank, the United Nations Development Programme (UNDP) and the United Nations Environment Programme (UNEP) (sections 5.4, 5.5). There may also be strong links between regional and sub-regional treaties or initiatives and an MEA in that all may relate to a global concern. The conservation of biological diversity in Africa

---

1 Rachel Carson, *Silent Spring* (Mariner Books, 2002). Originally published in 1962, *Silent Spring* alerted the world to the negative environmental and health consequences of the use of pesticides and herbicides in particular; Donella H. Meadows, Denis L. Meadows, Jørgen Randers and William W. Behrens III, *Limits to Growth* (Pan Books, 1974). *Limits to Growth* was originally published in 1972. The research for the study was conducted at the Massachusetts Institute of Technology and sponsored by the Club of Rome, an NGO. The study, based on the systems dynamic modelling techniques available at the time, pointed to the incapacity of the Earth to accommodate ongoing economic and population growth. Both publications received significant criticism especially on account of the methodologies used, but their messages sounded through in policy circles, even if not always in subsequent policies.

is the focus of, for example, the Biodiversity Convention, the African Nature Conservation Convention and KAZA.

As mentioned above, global concerns are at the basis of the environmental summits that have been held under the auspices of the United Nations. The first of these summits was the Stockholm Conference, held in 1972. While the intention had been to organize a world summit, due to the Cold War the conference was boycotted by most states associated with the Soviet bloc, with only Romania and Yugoslavia attending. It was during the preparations for the Stockholm Conference that developing states first forcefully articulated their environmental concerns as related to poverty. They challenged the then predominant conceptualization of environmental problems as resulting from industrial development and solvable by the application of increased scientific knowledge and new technological developments and asserted that poverty was also among the causes of environmental degradation. They thereby highlighted the North–South dimension of environmental policy and law (section 2.4). The Stockholm Conference resulted in the adoption of the 1972 Stockholm Declaration on the Human Environment (Stockholm Declaration) and the Action Plan for the Human Environment and encouraged the adoption of several MEAs[2] as well as the establishment of UNEP by the United Nations General Assembly (UNGA) in 1972 (UNGA Res. 2997(XXVII)). Even if developing states voiced their concerns regarding the relationship between poverty and the environment the substantive focus of international environmental law continued to be on nature conservation and the prevention of pollution, evidenced by the more concrete policy measures adopted at, and the MEAs resulting from, the Stockholm Conference.

Two subsequent landmark events in the development of international environmental policy and law were the 1987 Report of the World Commission on Environment and Development (WCED), also known as the Brundtland Commission,[3] and the 1992 United Nations Conference on Environment and Development (UNCED or Rio Conference). The WCED Report mainstreamed the term "sustainable development" and underscored the linkages between environment and

---

2 Examples are the 1972 London Convention on the Prevention of Pollution of the Marine Environment by Dumping of Wastes and Other Matter (London Convention), the World Heritage Convention and CITES.
3 WCED, *Our Common Future* (OUP, 1987).

development. UNCED resulted in the adoption of a number of new MEAs,[4] the 1992 Rio Declaration on Environment and Development (Rio Declaration) and an action plan, known as Agenda 21, as well as the non-legally binding 1992 Statement on Forests. UNCED also led to the establishment of the Commission on Sustainable Development (CSD), a subsidiary body of the United Nations Economic and Social Council (ECOSOC) (UNGA Res. 47/191 (1993) and ECOSOC Res. 1993/207). The Rio Declaration provides an authoritative overview of principles that are important in international environmental law (Chapter 4).

In 2002 the World Summit on Sustainable Development was held in Johannesburg. The World Summit's final document, the Johannesburg Declaration on Sustainable Development (Johannesburg Declaration), emphasizes the need to involve the private sector in addressing environmental problems and promotes the development of public-private partnerships.

In 2012 the Conference on Sustainable Development, also known as the Rio+20 Conference, was held in Rio de Janeiro. "The Future We Want", its final document, reiterates many of the commitments made at earlier summits, emphasizes the need to green the economy and recommends the creation of a high-level political body to replace the CSD. This body was established by UNGA in 2013 and is known as the High-level Political Forum on Sustainable Development (UNGA Res. 67/203 (2012) and UNGA Res. 67/290 (2013)). "The Future We Want" also foregrounds transparency, public participation and access to justice (section 4.7.5). It does so by referring to their importance in attaining sustainable development in its third operational section, after the section that sets out commitments and the section that assesses progress and identifies gaps.

The names of the successive summits illustrate a shift of focus, from the protection of the environment to attaining sustainable development. This shift marks a change in the conceptualization of environmental concerns, from technical problems to complex socio-economic problems that involve basic structures of society, including North–South relationships and the private sector. This shift in conceptualization is also reflected in the 2000 Millennium Development Goals (MDGs), adopted by the UNGA meeting at the level of heads of state

---

4 Examples are the UNFCCC, the Biodiversity Convention and the 1994 Desertification Convention.

and government to mark the turning of the millennium (UNGA Res. 55/2 (2002)). The MDGs emphasize the links between poverty, hunger, health, education and environmental sustainability and point to the need for partnerships involving a variety of actors in order to attain sustainable development. Based on the outcome of the Rio+20 Conference and building on the MDGs, a set of Sustainable Development Goals (SDGs) were adopted by the UNGA in September 2015 (UNGA Res. 70/1 (2015)), which focus on attaining sustainable development and in that context on the protection of the environment.

2.4   North–South relations

As illustrated above, colonial relationships marked the early beginnings of international environmental law (section 2.2.1). However, as the previous section illustrated, North–South relations have continued to play a prominent role in the development of international environmental law, with developing states forcefully voicing their concerns during the negotiations for the Stockholm Conference (section 2.3). These negotiations took place when most developing states had attained independence and had started advocating the establishment of a New International Economic Order (NIEO). In pursuit of a NIEO, developing states sought, among other things, control over the natural resources within their territories (instead of these being controlled by foreign companies), the alleviation of poverty, the establishment of more legitimate international institutions in which they would have a greater say commensurate to their numbers and a more equitable distribution of wealth. This context impacted the preparations for the Stockholm Conference, in which developing states expressed their dissatisfaction with the one-sided framing of environmental problems as involving pollution emanating from industrialization. They advocated a socio-economic understanding of environmental problems that recognizes that both poverty and prosperity may have negative environmental consequences. Developing states also emphasized that without development the environmental problems of the South would persist and cautioned that a one-sided focus on environmental concerns related to pollution could harm development.

Developing states threatened to leave the Stockholm preparatory negotiating process when they found that their concerns did not receive sufficient recognition. A series of special negotiations on the topics of concern to developing states ensued, resulting in the 1971 Founex

Report on Development and Environment. This report formulated the position of developing states, using among others the following terms:

> However, the major environmental problems of developing countries are essentially of a different kind. They are predominantly problems that reflect the poverty and very lack of development of their societies. They are problems, in other words, of both rural and urban poverty. In both the towns and in the countryside, not merely the "quality of life", but life itself is endangered by poor water, housing, sanitation and nutrition, by sickness and disease and by natural disasters. These are problems, no less than those of industrial pollution, that clamour for attention in the context of the concern with human environment. They are problems which affect the greater mass of mankind.[para. 1.4]

> . . . Furthermore, it must be emphasized in all international forums, including the Stockholm Conference, that it is for the developed countries to reassure the developing world that their growing environmental concern will not hurt the continued development of the developing world nor would it be used to reduce resource transfers or to distort aid priorities or to adopt more protectionist policies or to insist on unrealistic environmental standards in the appraisal of development projects.[para. 4.12]

While these concerns found their way into the Stockholm Declaration, which reflects a broad conceptualization of environmental problems, the more concrete measures adopted at the meeting focused on the prevention of pollution. Thus, after the Stockholm Conference concerns regarding the lack of attention to the position of developing states remained.[5]

A more socio-economic understanding of environmental problems in terms of North–South relations found reflection in the Rio Declaration and the MEAs adopted at and after the Rio Conference. Developing states' concerns about the legitimacy of international decision-making processes, however, persisted. This was evidenced by developing states' initial rejection of the Global Environment Facility (GEF), as the financial mechanism for the UNFCCC and the Biodiversity Convention, because it was solely controlled by the World Bank, an organization in which developing states have limited influence (section 5.5).

---

5 See, Independent Commission on International Development Issues, *North-South: A Programme for Survival* (Pan Books, 1980) and the South Commission, *The Challenge to the South* (OUP, 1990).

Another important outcome of the Rio negotiating process in terms of North–South relations is the principle of common but differentiated responsibilities (section 4.5.7). It significantly strengthened the position of developing states by enabling them to bring to the table arguments that relate their situation of underdevelopment to the legacy of colonialism and to the unequal distribution of wealth across the globe. The principle provides a justification for the inclusion of financial mechanisms in MEAs and the establishment of international funding mechanisms such as the renegotiated GEF (section 5.5). One of the big challenges currently facing North–South relations is related to the principle of common but differentiated responsibilities. It concerns the implications of the principle for the position of emerging economies, such as Brazil, China, India and South Africa, in MEAs. These states now contribute significantly more to environmental problems than they used to and their capacity to fund sustainable development has increased. It is in this context that the question is being posed whether emerging economies should take on obligations beyond those that rest on other developing states. In other words, the question negotiators are faced with is whether differentiation between developing states is in line with the principle of common but differentiated responsibilities. Such further differentiation now seems to have been accepted in the negotiating process for the Paris Agreement, the successor for the Kyoto Protocol (section 3.4.3).

Another major challenge for international environmental law in the North–South context concerns the position of least developed states. Many of these states, in Africa in particular, are facing multiple environmental threats. These threats include droughts, floods and depletion of natural resources, in addition to threats emanating from armed conflicts. A phenomenon known as "land grabbing" exacerbates the problems that local populations face. "Land grabbing" involves the depletion of natural resources by foreign or local companies involved in large-scale commercial agricultural activities. As a result of these activities local populations are regularly left without access to land or water and thereby deprived of their livelihood. The question that arises with respect to the multiple problems faced by least developed states concerns the nature of the responsibility that other states and the international community have in addressing these problems. A similar question arises very poignantly in relation to small island states which, as a result of climate change-induced sea level rise, might disappear or become unsuitable for human habitation.

2.5   The roles of actors other than states

While states continue to be important actors in international environmental law, they are not the only actors engaged in normative development and executive decision-making. As illustrated above, NGOs have been and continue to be important actors in the development of international environmental law (section 2.2.2). In addition to NGOs, international organizations, private sector actors and sub-national entities also play important roles. This section illustrates how these actors influence the development and application of international environmental law.

UNEP through its Montevideo Programme for the Development and Periodic Review of Environmental Law, in which both state representatives and environmental law experts participate, contributes to the development of international environmental law. Since 1982, under this programme UNEP has adopted ten-year work plans that focus on distinct environmental law themes. Montevideo I specifically addressed the development of international environmental law; Montevideo IV, which runs from 2010 to 2020, focuses on the following themes: the effectiveness of environmental law; conservation, management and sustainable use of natural resources; challenges for environmental law; and the relationships with other fields of law. Other international organizations also impact the development of international environmental law by standard setting. In particular, IDBs, such as the World Bank and regional development banks, set standards for projects that they finance. Such standards focus on, for example, environmental impact assessment or public participation. Within the World Bank, as well as many other IDBs, these standards are incorporated in so-called OP&Ps which are binding for World Bank staff in their project-related work and can be the basis for the submission of a complaint to the World Bank Inspection Panel (section 6.4.1).

NGOs and private sector actors as observers at international negotiating conferences impact the development of international environmental law and thereby participate in normative development. The ISF and IUCN, for example, participate in negotiations at the International Maritime Organization (IMO); COP-20 (2014) of the UNFCCC was attended by representatives of 624 NGOs and COP-16 (2013) of CITES was attended by 60 international and over one hundred national NGOs. Actors with observer status at these meetings generally may submit documents and may be given the floor but they do not have voting rights.

NGOs and private sector actors also have developed their own regulatory approaches and participate directly in instruments that seek to implement international environmental law. The certification schemes operated by the FSC provide an example of the former. The FSC is a multi-stakeholder organization, composed of environmental and social NGOs and private sector stakeholders. It was established in 1993, after the Rio Conference failed to adopt an MEA on forests, adopting instead the Statement on Forests. Private sector organizations and NGOs thus sought and found another means of promoting sustainable forest management, that is, certification. Within the FSC certification process both normative development and executive decision-making are engaged in. The former involves developing the certification standards and procedures; the latter the application of those standards and procedures to individual wood producers and products for purposes of certification. Similar to the FSC, the Marine Stewardship Council (MSC), also a multi-stakeholder organization, operates certification schemes for marine fish products. The financial support that WWF provides to KAZA is an example of an NGO directly participating in and supporting an instrument that seeks to implement international environmental law (section 2.3). WWF's participation and support in KAZA is subject to WWF policies such as its policy on community-based natural resource management (CBNRM) in Southern Africa. CBNRM is based on, among other principles, the principle that "[t]he community or group that lives with the resource should also be the same as the group that makes the decisions over the resource and the same as the group that benefits" (CBNRM 2006). WWF thereby influences norms on public participation in decision-making and on the distribution of benefits and thus participates in normative development. When WWF applies these norms to concrete situations, it participates in executive decision-making.

Private sector actors also participate in the so-called flexible mechanisms, such as the CDM, established by the Kyoto Protocol and in the Prototype Carbon Fund (PCF), established by the World Bank in order to facilitate the transfer of funds from developed to developing states under the climate regime (section 5.5). In the CDM private sector actors execute projects in developing states and are involved in the certification of CERs emanating from these projects. In the PCF, companies and states invest resources used to finance climate change projects in developing states and both types of actors participate in decision-making in the Fund, commensurate to the size of their investment. They thereby co-determine the rules applicable to projects supported by the Fund.

The largest scale initiative to involve the private sector in implementing environmental, but also human rights, labour and anti-corruption, standards is probably the United Nations Global Compact, an initiative launched by the United Nations in July 2000. It counts over 12,000 corporate and other stakeholder members from 170 states. The Global Compact seeks to further corporate responsibility on the basis of ten principles derived from international environmental, human rights, labour and anti-corruption instruments and by identifying best practices, for example in the area of climate change. The three environmental principles that inform the Global Compact are the precautionary approach, the promotion of environmental responsibility and the development and diffusion of environmentally friendly technologies.

Sub-national actors also cooperate across state borders and may directly engage with other international actors. The C40 Cities Climate Leadership Group provides an example. It is an initiative of a group of large cities, also known as global cities, and aims to address climate change in cities, through collaboration and knowledge sharing. C40 cooperates with UNEP, for example, on a solid waste reduction programme in order to reduce methane outputs. The Western Climate Initiative Inc. is an example of cooperation between states of the United States and Canadian provinces in the area of climate change. The Western Climate Initiative Inc. is a non-profit organization that aims to establish a compliance tracking system for GHG emissions. In Europe, transboundary cooperation between municipalities and other local actors is also taking place, for example within the framework of the nature conservation area known as the Rode Beek/Rodebach, in which a Dutch municipality, water board and nature conservation organization cooperate with a German municipality. Within the European Union such projects may receive support from funding mechanisms, such as the European Regional Development Fund, which supported the Rode Beek/Rodebach project. Such initiatives can also be institutionalized under the 2006 EU Regulation on European Grouping of Territorial Cooperation (Regulation (EC) No. 1082/2006) as a result of which they can attain legal personality under European Union law, with the applicable law being that of the member state of registry.

2.6 Assessment

While international environmental law can be characterized by continuity in that approaches developed in the past are built upon and further developed, this chapter also illustrates changes that have taken place in international environmental law over time. These changes concern in particular the broadening of the substantive focus of international environmental law and the reconceptualization of environmental problems. At the same time the role of non-state actors has changed.

The substantive focus of international environmental law initially, in the late nineteenth and early twentieth centuries, was on nature conservation, in particular the protection of valuable species in African colonies, and transboundary issues involving a small number of states. During the second half of the twentieth century that focus broadened to include the need to address pollution of rivers, oceans and the atmosphere more broadly, as evidenced by the LRTAP Convention and regional seas conventions adopted at the time (section 5.2.4). The environmental problems addressed by these instruments were regarded as solvable through increased scientific knowledge and new technological developments. In the Northern Hemisphere, technological innovation indeed did result in better protection of the environment, if we consider, for example, the success of the LRTAP Convention in reducing acid rain, as well as other regional instruments (section 3.4.1) adopted at the time. The success of these instruments is closely related to the introduction of new technologies. During the latter part of the twentieth century international environmental law increasingly sought to address the global social and economic dimensions of environmental problems and the use of natural resources. As a result, environmental problems have been re-conceptualized as socio-economic problems which are of global concern. This change is captured by the term sustainable development.

At the same time, international organizations, NGOs and the private sector have become engaged in normative development and executive decision-making. Think of IDBs, which develop and apply OP&Ps, WWF's involvement in KAZA, the FSC, in which NGOs and the private sector cooperate, and the PCF, in which states and the private sector cooperate.

Concomitant to the above-mentioned developments, the understanding of what is at stake in international environmental law, that is what needs to be regulated and how it needs to be regulated, also evolved. The next chapter discusses how different types of international regulatory regimes have developed over time and become part of international law.

3   Evolving insights about what is at stake

3.1   Introduction

This chapter traces how insights about what ought to be addressed by international environmental law have evolved over time and how these insights have affected the content of contemporary instruments and regulatory approaches. The focus in this chapter will be on how international environmental law has evolved since roughly the 1970s. As section 2.2.1 illustrates, the insight that species and habitats may require protection emerged at around the turn of the nineteenth century. As of the 1940s, and especially since the 1960s, the insight emerged that polluting substances should be kept out of the environment, or at least that their presence in the environment should be limited. Since roughly the 1970s, this insight started to leave its mark on international environmental law. Initially the focus was on the development of regulatory regimes that address inputs of polluting substances into the environment. More recently the focus also has been on the development of regimes that address trade in hazardous substances. Even more recently, the insight that we need to focus on ecosystems and ecosystem-based governance approaches has also emerged and started to influence international environmental law. Furthermore, the insight that we may be living in an epoch, referred to as the Anthropocene, where humans are influencing the Earth's systems such as the ozone layer and the climate system poses new challenges for contemporary international environmental law.

This chapter treats the following themes: responding to and preventing accidental pollution; responding to and preventing operational pollution; addressing trade in hazardous substances; ecosystem-based governance; and the Anthropocene. Prior to engaging with these themes, this chapter first discusses how harmful substances enter the environment and how human activities otherwise may disturb the environment.

3.2   Harmful substances, disturbances and the environment

Environmentally harmful substances, or pollutants, emanate from a host of different human activities including agriculture, industrial production processes, mining, transportation, medical treatment, household activities and the generation of energy from fossil fuels or nuclear sources. Pollutants may be contained in, for example, cooling liquids for refrigerators; fertilizers, pesticides and herbicides used in agriculture; paint used on the hulls of ships to prevent marine micro-organisms from attaching themselves to the hull (known as fouling, hence anti-fouling paint), aerosols used in spray-cans, packaging material and waste as well as decommissioned products such as ships and electronic equipment. These substances then are useful and harmful at the same time, in the sense that they perform a function valued by humans and may harm human health and the environment. Harmful substances may pollute soil, air, atmosphere, groundwater, surface waters and marine waters and as a result harm ecosystems and the Earth's systems such as the climate system.

Polluting substances enter the environment due to accidents that may occur during the production, transportation or use of harmful substances or the products of which they are a part. In addition, pollutants enter the environment as a by-product of the use of harmful substances or the products of which they are a part and through a variety of production processes and activities. The former is referred to as accidental pollution; the latter as operational pollution. While accidental pollution often attracts widespread attention, operational pollution is by far the bigger contributor to environmental degradation.

Noise and light pollution also may have significant effects on the environment. For example, the use of sonar at sea has been associated with disturbances in communication between marine mammals, in particular whales, as well as interfering with their feeding patterns. Light pollution has been associated, among other things, with the disruption of circadian (24-hour) cycles, affecting feeding patterns in some species, and with disturbing the navigation systems of migrating birds. Night time light furthermore has been linked to reduced production of melatonin, which has been associated with increased risk of cancer, both in rats and human shift-workers. In addition, both noise and light pollution hamper human enjoyment of the outdoors.

Ecosystems are also disturbed by humans taking or using substances from the environment and by the introduction of foreign species. Taking parts of the environment for human use may involve activities such as hunting and fishing for human consumption, collecting plants for medicinal use or clearing forests to use the trees as timber or the cleared land for agricultural purposes. It may also involve using surface water as a cooling liquid in industrial processes or marine water for ballasting ships. Water that has been used as a cooling liquid when released into the environment may have a higher temperature than the receiving aquatic environment or may carry (residues of) harmful substances used in the production process and as a result pollute the receiving aquatic ecosystem. Ships take on board ballast water at one location at sea and de-ballast in another ocean area, after a voyage when the ship is approaching its destination for re-loading. As a consequence, ocean water and the marine organisms that it contains are transferred from one marine ecosystem to another.[1] It is believed that seawater taken on board in the western North Atlantic Ocean and released in the Black Sea in the 1980s led to the introduction of a jellyfish (*Mnemiopsis leidy*), in the Black Sea. Conditions of high nutrient availability and overfishing apparently enabled the jellyfish to thrive and dominate the Black Sea ecosystem. The flourishing of jellyfish, also native ones, today is a more widespread phenomenon that has been linked to the dire state of many marine ecosystems.

While the introduction of foreign species in marine ecosystems through de-ballasting is a by-product of an economic activity, such introductions have also been actively pursued by humans for economic reasons. The introduction of the Nile Perch in Lake Victoria, starting in the 1950s, provides an example with far reaching detrimental consequences for the ecosystem of the lake. As the Nile Perch thrived, other species declined and the ecosystem of the lake became less diverse. It also led to the development of an economically lucrative fishery especially for export purposes, the fish apparently being too expensive for the local population. More recently, the use of genetically modified plants in agriculture has also become the subject of debate. The debate concerns the question whether the introduction of genetically modified crop plants may negatively affect non-genetically modified crop plants, naturally growing plants and human health.

---

1 This issue is now addressed by the 2004 Ballast Water Convention, adopted under the auspices of the IMO.

The environment has a carrying capacity, which is the capacity of an ecosystem to assimilate substances and adapt to disturbances. Think of, for example, the capacity of wetlands to remove nutrients from polluted waters and the ability of birds to adapt their vocalizations to the noise levels of urban environments. Destructive events such as fires may also be part of the natural regenerating process of some ecosystems. For example, in Australia, forests populated by Mountain Ash (*Eucalyptus regnans*) require fire to regenerate because the fire causes its fruits to open. These fruits hold the seeds that rejuvenate the forest.

The carrying capacity of the environment depends on the state of the ecosystem in question and the nature and quantity of the substance or disturbance. Resilient ecosystems are more likely to assimilate substances and accommodate disturbances and natural substances are more likely to be assimilated without negative consequences than synthetic ones. In terms of synthetic substances and their consequences the plastics circulating the world's oceans provide a pertinent example. These plastics consist of, among other components, small non-biodegradable particles of plastic, including nanoparticles contained in, for example, cosmetics such as sunscreen. These particles are ingested by planktonic organisms, fish, marine mammals and birds and interfere with their digestion. Concerns also relate to the effects of chemical additives that may leach out of the plastic particles and waterborne pollutants, including persistent organic pollutants (POPs), which may adhere to these particles. It is feared that these substances may negatively affect the ingesting organism, their reproduction, their prey and thus the food chain.

Relying on the carrying capacity of ecosystems to assimilate pollutants and accommodate disturbances has proven to be problematic because the effects of pollutants and disturbances in the environment often have not been or cannot be properly factored into policies and laws. This problem is exacerbated by the fact that any ecosystem is likely to be affected by multiple pollutants and disturbances and over lengthy periods of time. In other words, predicting the carrying capacity of the environment has proven to be very difficult if not impossible. As a result, degradation of the environment due to human activity has often come as a surprise. The discovery of the hole in the ozone layer above Antarctica in 1985 is a case in point (section 3.4.2).

The hole in the ozone layer and human-induced climate change point to a further challenge that international environmental law faces: the fact that human activities are affecting essential Earth's systems, such as the ozone layer and the climate system. This awareness has prompted the call for the denomination of a new epoch in the Earth's history: the Anthropocene. The term Anthropocene implies that the influence of humankind on the Earth's systems is now on par with the impact of forces of nature and is co-shaping the history of the Earth (section 3.7).

3.3   Responding to and preventing accidental pollution

As mentioned above, environmentally harmful substances may enter the environment as a result of accidents, brought on by natural calamities or human failure. Accidents often induce the adoption of new or the revision of existing international instruments with the aim of in future preventing or, at least, better addressing accidents. Note that instruments adopted in the aftermath of accidents may also serve to address operational pollution from the same source. This section addresses how nuclear accidents, shipping accidents and industrial accidents have affected the development of international instruments.

3.3.1   Nuclear accidents

The 2011 calamity at the nuclear plants at Fukushima, Japan, provides an example of how accidents may foster the development of international environmental law. It led the International Atomic Energy Agency (IAEA) to adopt the 2011 IAEA Action Plan on Nuclear Safety which, among other things, calls for the review and strengthening of IAEA safety standards and for the establishment of a global nuclear liability regime. The revision of IAEA standards was concluded in 2012. It led to minor amendments of the standards and the finding that these standards should remain under scrutiny of the existing periodic review and revision process.

The reference to the global liability regime concerns a long-standing problem related to the fact that two international regimes on civil liability for compensation of nuclear damage exist. One regime is based at the IAEA. It encompasses the 1963 Vienna Convention on Civil Liability for Nuclear Damage and the 1997 Protocol to Amend the 1963 Vienna Convention on Civil Liability for Nuclear Damage. These instruments are open to all member states of the United Nations. The second regime is based at the Organisation for Economic Cooperation and Development (OECD). It encompasses the 1960 Paris Convention on Third Party Liability in the Field of Nuclear Energy and its 1963

Brussels Supplementary Convention. These instruments are open to OECD member states and to states whose participation in the instruments has been approved by the contracting parties to the OECD instruments. The 1988 Joint Protocol relating to both the Paris and the Vienna Conventions aims to bridge the gap between the two regimes by entitling victims in the territory of a state party to one regime to the rights provided by the other regime. In other words, an operator of a nuclear plant in the territory of a party to one of the regimes will be liable according to the rules of that regime for damage caused in the territory of a party to the other regime.

The two liability regimes also faced criticism from non-nuclear power generating states for not taking their interests sufficiently into account. The 1997 Convention on Supplementary Compensation for Nuclear Damage (Supplementary Convention), adopted within the IAEA, aims to address these criticisms by further defining nuclear damage to include, among other things, the cost of measures to repair harm to the environment, preventive measures and a certain degree of economic loss (Art. I(6)) and by increasing the guaranteed amount of compensation that is available (Art. III). The Supplementary Convention is a self-standing agreement, meaning that if widely ratified, it would result in a unified regime for civil liability for nuclear damage, without a state having to become a party to the IAEA or OECD-based regimes, referred to above. Given that the Supplementary Convention has not entered into force, the process of bridging the two regimes is still ongoing and within the context of the above-mentioned 2011 IAEA Action Plan resulted in the recommendation that nuclear power and non-nuclear power-producing states adhere to a global nuclear liability regime.

The IAEA's express engagement with environmental aspects of nuclear energy was also triggered by a nuclear accident: the 1986 calamity at Chernobyl, Ukraine (then part of the Union of Soviet Socialist Republics (USSR)). This calamity reoriented the organization from focusing mainly on stimulating the availability of the benefits of nuclear technology throughout the world, to include in its regulations the possible adverse impacts of nuclear technology on the environment.[2] In addition to the instruments mentioned so far, the IAEA has

---

2 In the aftermath of Chernobyl the following conventions were adopted by the IAEA: 1986 Notification Convention; 1986 Assistance Convention; 1994 Safety Convention; 1997 Joint Convention on Spent Fuel and Radioactive Waste. In addition, during this period the 1980 Convention on the Protection of Nuclear Material entered into force.

also adopted a large number of recommendations, safety standards and codes of conduct that address accidental and operational pollution emanating from the use of nuclear substances.

3.3.2 Shipping accidents

Conventions related to nuclear energy are not the only ones that can be traced to accidents; a number of treaties that address both accidental and operational marine pollution from ships have a similar origin. In this respect the names of the *Titanic, Torrey Canyon, Amoco Cadiz* and *Exxon Valdez* stand out.

The origin of the 1974 Convention on the Safety of Life at Sea (SOLAS Convention) is to be found in a precursor adopted in 1914, after the sinking of the *Titanic* in 1912. The SOLAS Convention provides standards for the construction, equipment and operation of ships in order to secure seaworthiness; it therefore does not directly address the protection of the marine environment. The SOLAS Convention, like other treaties administered by the IMO, instead addresses safety at sea and thereby indirectly serves to protect the marine environment. Other relevant IMO conventions include those regarding the prevention of collisions at sea (COLREG) and the standards of training, certification and watchkeeping for seafarers (STCW Convention). Also relevant in this respect is the 2006 Maritime Labour Convention adopted under the auspices of the International Labour Organization (ILO), which brought together and modernized various ILO instruments related to maritime labour conditions that had been adopted over time.

The 1967 *Torrey Canyon* accident, off the Cornish coast in the English Channel, led to the adoption of the 1969 Intervention Convention. In 1973, it was supplemented by a protocol that brought substances other than oil within its remit.[3] The Intervention Convention introduced the entitlement of coastal states to interfere with a foreign flag ship on the high seas – normally subject to flag state jurisdiction – if a ship by virtue of pollution or threat of pollution of the sea constitutes a "grave or imminent danger" to its coastline or related interests. This entitlement has been incorporated in Article 221(1) of the 1982 Convention on the Law of the Sea (LOS Convention) subject to the lower threshold of "actual or threatened damage" that "may reasonably be expected to result in major harmful consequences". At the source of the

---

3 1973 Protocol to the Intervention Convention.

Intervention Convention are the United Kingdom's doubts about the legality of its action when it bombed the *Torrey Canyon* to avoid worse environmental damage from occurring. In addition to the Intervention Convention, the *Torrey Canyon* accident also provided impetus for the development of civil liability regimes for accidental vessel source pollution, both of a public and private nature.[4] It also led to the initial negotiations of what eventually would be the 73/78 Convention for the Prevention of Marine Pollution from Ships (MARPOL Convention). The MARPOL Convention, replacing the OILPOL Convention (section 2.3), provides the global framework for controlling vessel source pollution on the basis of its six annexes, which contain specific regulations and have been developed over time. Its annexes address the prevention of pollution by oil, noxious liquid substances carried in bulk, harmful substances carried in packaged form, sewage from ships, garbage from ships and air pollution from ships. Annexes I and II on respectively oil pollution and on noxious liquid substances carried in bulk, are mandatory, while the other annexes may be ratified by a state after it becomes a party to the MARPOL Convention. The MARPOL Convention is an example of an instrument that although adopted in the aftermath of an accident, addresses operational pollution.

The 1978 *Amoco Cadiz* accident, off the Atlantic coast of France, led to questions about the then time practice of salvors working under a "no cure, no pay" formula contained in the Lloyd's Standard Form of Salvage Agreement, also known as the Lloyd's Open Form. Based on this arrangement the cure and the guarantee for payment were the salvaged ship and its cargo. The *Amoco Cadiz* accident, however, illustrated that it was not only the value of the ship and its cargo that were at stake in a salvage operation but also the protection of the environment and related interests – in this case the value of the ship and cargo was under half the total amount of the final award, the rest being related to damage claims originating in pollution. In other words, third

---

4 The 1969 Civil Liability Convention and the 1971 Fund Convention, were adopted under the auspices of the IMO in the aftermath of the *Torrey Canyon* accident. They were significantly revised in 1992 by protocols, which entered into force in 1996. The private sector civil liability regimes adopted in the aftermath of the accident were the 1966 Tanker Owners Voluntary Agreement concerning Liability for Oil Pollution also known as TOVALOP and the 1971 Supplementary Convention to TOVALOP. These two agreements were not renewed after the entry into force of the 1992 protocols. The IMO civil liability regime for carriage of oil was supplemented by the 1996 Convention on Liability and Compensation for Damage in Connection with the Carriage of Hazardous and Noxious Substances by Sea (HNS Convention). The HNS Convention is not in force, it has been superseded by a 2010 HNS Protocol, which has not entered into force either.

parties, including public and private actors, had an interest in the salvage operation. Yet the Lloyd's Open Form-based salvage contract did not provide compensation to the salvor if (s)he acted in the interest of these third parties, for example by avoiding an oil spill but losing the ship. In addition to the above-mentioned issues raised by the *Amoco Cadiz* and other shipping accidents during the 1970s and 1980s, it also became clear that courts would hold salvors liable for negligence resulting in environmental damage. These concerns and others regarding the state of the law of salvage led the IMO, through the *Comité Maritime International*, to develop the 1989 Salvage Convention. The Salvage Convention recognizes, among other things, that salvage operations can make a major contribution to public interests (maritime safety and the protection of the environment), that all parties involved in salvage operations have a duty of care to protect the environment, the right of coastal states to protect their interests during the salvage operation and that compensation for preventing environmental damage during the salvage operation may be awarded. In addition to these developments, the accident with the *Amoco Cadiz* also led to the adoption of the 1982 Paris Memorandum of Understanding (MOU) on Port State Control (Paris MOU on Port State Control). Based on this instrument maritime authorities in Western Europe agreed to collaborate by inspecting and if necessary detaining foreign ships in their harbours and by exchanging information about "suspicious" ships. The standards for inspection are international instruments concerning the safety and environmental conditions of ships, including IMO and ILO conventions. Port State Control regimes have now been adopted in most regions of the world (section 5.2.4).

The 1989 *Exxon Valdez* accident, in Prince William Sound, Alaska, led to the adoption of the 1990 OPRC Convention on preparedness, response and cooperation regarding oil spills related to shipping. It was supplemented by the 2000 OPRC-HNS Protocol, which brought hazardous and noxious substances within its ambit. The OPRC Convention requires flag states for their ships and port states and coastal states to have in place plans and equipment for dealing with shipping accidents, encourages states to cooperate in limiting environmental damage from these accidents and determines how the costs of such operations are to be defrayed. In other words, the OPRC Convention seeks to achieve that all parties involved in a shipping accident are better prepared to deal with its potential consequences than was the case when the *Exxon Valdez* hit a reef in Prince William Sound.

3.3.3 Industrial accidents

While nuclear and shipping accidents have elicited the responses discussed above, industrial calamities in general have not led to similar international normative developments. Calamities such as at the
Union Carbide chemical plant in Bhopal, India, in 1984, which due
to gas leakage caused thousands of deaths and immediate injuries as
well as thousands of long-term injuries, remain unaddressed by international environmental law. Instead, the harm suffered tends to be
considered before national courts in home states (that is, where the
company is incorporated) and host states (in other words, where the
activities of the company are undertaken), often to little avail.

The different approaches to the regulation of accidents related to
nuclear energy-producing plants and maritime transportation of dangerous substances, on the one hand, and industrial calamities in general, on the other hand, raise several points that link into ongoing
debates on matters of justice in international environmental law. First,
from a traditional international law perspective international environmental law does not address industrial accidents such as in Bhopal
because they are less likely to have transboundary consequences for
the territory of other states or areas beyond natural jurisdiction. This
argument finds support in the regional 1992 Industrial Accidents
Convention, adopted within the UNECE. It applies only to "industrial
accidents capable of causing transboundary effects" (Art. 2(1)). Second,
from a political-economy perspective the deficient manner in which
the Bhopal calamity was addressed occurs in particular in developing
states, with the companies involved being incorporated in or having
strong links with companies incorporated in developed states, which
may be why international environmental law does not address these
calamities. Third, industrial catastrophes such as Bhopal illustrate the
normative relevance of taking a transnational approach to environmental problems. That such an approach is possible is illustrated by
the so-called Seveso directives adopted in the European Union, which
apply regardless of potential transboundary effects.[5] Fourth, these considerations are not only relevant to calamities such as Bhopal, but also
to calamities which find their origin in systemic operational and accidental pollution such as those associated with, for example, the past

---

5 The first Seveso Directive was adopted in reaction to an accident that happened in 1976 at a
chemical plant in Seveso, Italy. It has been regularly updated in view of new accidents, including
in Europe but also the Bhopal calamity. The latest Seveso Directive is the so-called Seveso III
Directive (Directive 2012/18/EU).

operations of Shell in Ogoniland, Nigeria, between 1958 and 1993, and those of Chevron/Texaco in Ecuador during roughly the same period (section 7.5).

3.4 Responding to and preventing operational pollution

Responses to operational pollution have often been informed by the environment signalling that its carrying capacity has been reached. Examples are discovery of the hole in the ozone layer in 1985, the link between the acidification of lakes in Scandinavia and sulphur emissions in continental Europe established during the 1970s and the state of the river Rhine in the 1980s. The climate change regime is perhaps an exception as the UNFCCC was adopted when the causes of climate change were still highly debated, although it is now generally agreed that human-induced climate change is a fact.

This section discusses a number of regulatory approaches that have been used to address operational pollution. It concentrates on the introduction of best available technology (BAT) and best environmental practices (BEP), with a focus on how these policies evolved in Europe, and on the banning and phasing out of substances, with a focus on the regimes that address the dumping of wastes at sea and the emission of ozone-depleting substances.

3.4.1 Introducing best available technology and best environmental practices

As mentioned above, operational pollution is incidental to a production process or an activity. It may originate from a, so-called, point or diffuse source. Point sources are typically outlets that can be identified as the point where a pollutant enters the environment. Diffuse sources of pollution reach the environment in particular by seeping into the soil, groundwater, larger water systems and eventually the marine environment. They are associated especially with the use of fertilizers as well as pesticides and herbicides in agriculture. A diffuse source may be turned into a point source by, for example, the construction of a sewage system with an outlet to the marine environment. During the nineteenth century the introduction of underground sewage systems and (ever higher) smokestacks were means of dealing with pollution. It later emerged that these innovations were also problematic as they led to the displacement of pollutants over large distances – sulphur emissions in continental Europe and the United States leading to acidification of lakes in, respectively, Scandinavia and Canada[6] – and into other components of the environment – nutrients in sewage transposed from local environments to the marine environment, contributing to algal blooms. How the reduction of pollutants from point and diffuse sources might be regulated will be discussed based on experience in Europe with regard to the reduction of pollution in watercourses[7] and of land-based sources of marine pollution in the Northeast Atlantic.[8]

During the 1970s relevant forums in Europe addressed point sources through so-called end-of-pipeline technology, involving discharge limits and the installation of filters at the end of the emitting source (the pipeline), and diffuse sources through setting environmental quality standards. However, end-of-pipeline technology and environmental quality standards were found to be problematic because they do not address the root causes of pollution. End-of-pipeline technology furthermore generates waste (for example, filters). Both point and diffuse sources, therefore, increasingly were addressed by regulations that focus on the production processes or the activities themselves. This change of focus resulted in requirements to apply the BAT for point source and BEP for diffuse sources. BAT measures indicate the technology or substances that are best used in certain production process, an example being the production of emulsion polyvinyl chloride (PVC).[9] BEP measures address how certain activities are best carried out; an example is reducing the use of pesticides by changing agricultural practices.[10] These sector-specific measures are at present combined with ecosystem-based management approaches, including environmental quality standards, (section 3.6). In Europe this development is stimulated by two European Union directives: the Water Framework Directive and the Marine Strategy Framework Directive,

---

6 This problem was addressed by the LRTAP Convention.

7 See in particular the 1999 Rhine Convention, replacing a number of earlier treaties also focused on the protection of the Rhine, the earliest of which dates back to 1963.

8 1992 OSPAR Convention, focused on the protection of the marine environment of the Northeast Atlantic Ocean, and its predecessor where land-based sources are concerned, the 1974 Paris Convention.

9 For an example see OSPAR Recommendation 99/1 on the Best Available Techniques for the Manufacture of Emulsion PVC (e PVC).

10 For an example see OSPAR Recommendation 2000/1 on Best Environmental Practice for the Reduction of Inputs of Agricultural Pesticides to the Environment through the Use of Integrated Crop Management Techniques.

both of which require ecosystem-based approaches, of which BAT, BEP and other measures are a part.[11]

3.4.2   Banning or phasing out substances or activities

Operational pollution is also limited by prohibiting the use of substances or activities. An example of a prohibition to use a substance is the ban on the use of harmful organotins in anti-fouling paints, used on the hulls of ships, contained in the 2001 Anti-fouling Convention. Another example is the 2001 Stockholm Convention, which aims to phase out the use of POPs.[12] The main elements of the Stockholm Convention are: a list of, initially 12, POPs that are to be phased out by eliminating their production, use, import and export (Art. 3; Annex A(elimination)/Annex B(restriction)); a system of exceptions that a state may enter onto a convention-based public registry when it becomes a party to the convention and which will allow it, by way of exception, to continue to import and use specific POPs – such exceptions expire after a period of five years unless they are properly motivated (Art. 4); and measures on how to deal with stockpiles of, and wastes containing, POPs, including their import for environmentally sound disposal (Art. 6). A similar system is used by the 2013 Minamata Convention to phase out products containing mercury or its components (Arts. 4, 6). It does so in combination with the application of a prior informed consent procedure for trade in mercury or its compounds (section 3.5) and the prescription of BAT and BEP for emissions of mercury.

An example of a prohibited activity is the ban on the incineration of wastes at sea, initially included in a 1993 decision of the COP of the London Convention. The 1996 Protocol to the London Convention incorporated this ban into the text of the convention and introduced the so-called "reverse listing" approach for the dumping of wastes at sea. "Reverse listing" in this context means that those substances that may be dumped at sea are listed, instead of those that may not be dumped at sea. As a result, new substances are automatically covered by the ban. This approach contrasts with that of the original London

---

11 Directive 2000/60/EC establishing a framework for Community action in the field of water policy and Directive 2008/56/EC establishing a framework for Community action in the field of marine environmental policy.

12 The Stockholm Convention was preceded at the regional level by the so-called 1998 POPs Protocol to the LRTAP Convention.

Convention, which listed those substances or groups of substances whose dumping was prohibited, thereby requiring a decision as to whether a substance should be banned from dumping every time a new substance or new group of substances came on the market.

A regime that is generally acknowledged as having been successful at banning the use of certain substances is the ozone regime. It consists of the 1985 Vienna Convention on the Ozone Layer and its 1987 Montreal Protocol. The ozone layer is an atmospheric layer that shields the Earth against over-exposure from ultraviolet radiation in sunlight. As mentioned above, the "ozone hole" above Antarctica was discovered in 1985 (section 3.2). However, suspicions that the ozone layer was thinning had been voiced earlier on and in 1985 it became clear that the depletion process had been ongoing since the 1970s.[13] The thinning of the ozone layer is caused by human-induced emissions of certain gases, including chlorofluorocarbons (CFCs), which were used in, among other things, cooling installations, spray-cans and in the production process for styrofoam. Scientists currently suggest that the ozone layer will take another 50 years to recover. The fact that many ozone-depleting substances are also GHGs entails that their reduction has contributed to addressing climate change. However, it also emerged that some of the substitutes for ozone-depleting substances were also GHGs. This situation points to the fragmented nature of international environmental law, it eventually led to cooperation between the climate change regime and the ozone regime. It is generally agreed that there are certain reasons for the success of the ozone regime. The most important reasons for success are probably that alternatives to ozone-depleting substances were available accompanied by the fact that the use of ozone-depleting substances involved a limited number of production processes and products. In addition, like-minded developed states took the lead in implementing the regime. These characteristics stand in sharp contrast to those faced by the climate change regime discussed below.

3.4.3   Internationally agreed emission reductions

The climate change regime more than any other regime illustrates the difficulty of changing the ways we do things when it comes to the core

---

13 J.C. Farman, B.G. Gardiner and J.D. Shanklin, "Large losses of total ozone in Antarctica reveal seasonal ClO$_x$/NO$_x$ interaction", 315 *Nature* (1985) 207–10; Jonathan Shanklin, "Reflections on the ozone hole", 465 *Nature* (2010) 34–5.

of our economic activity. Our economy is driven by the use of GHGs and in particular by the use of fossil fuels for the production of energy. About 70 per cent of all GHG emissions and 68 per cent of carbon dioxide (CO_2) emissions emanate from the combustion of fossil fuels to produce energy. In order to limit these emissions fundamental changes in energy production and consumption patterns will be required, given that an outright ban on the use of fossil fuels is not practicable.

Attaining the reduction of GHG emissions involves the vital interests of states and private parties. It involves the interests of fossil fuel-producing states such as a number of Middle Eastern states that rely heavily on the export of oil, but also Australia, which is an exporter of coal. It requires China to redirect its coal-based energy production to more sustainable sources. But, the sustainability of alternative sources are debated, leading to the contestation of investments in wind and solar power. Moreover, private actors engaged in carbon-based energy production run the risk of being left with fossil fuel-based "stranded assets" worth hundreds of billions, while they are being encouraged, often by way of subsidies, to also invest in renewable energy sources.

The Kyoto Protocol sought to address the challenges referred to above by imposing internationally agreed emission reduction obligations on developed and economy in transition states (Annex I states) and not on developing states (Art. 3, Annex I). Furthermore, it introduced market mechanisms, the so-called flexible mechanisms. These mechanisms enable Annex I states to cooperate among themselves in reducing emissions (Art. 6), Annex I states to invest in developing states in order to reduce emissions there, the so-called CDM, (Art. 12) and the introduction of a market in emission reduction units (Art. 17). Both public and private parties may participate in these mechanisms. Why might it be in the interests of a developed state or a private party linked to that state to invest in emission reductions in a developing state, instead of at home? Such an investment is of value to a developed state or a private party linked to that state because it is cheaper to reduce emissions in developing states, given that many developed states have introduced technologies to reduce emissions and that every step to further reduce emissions is likely to be more expensive. Moreover, the emission reduction units obtained by way of, for example, CDM projects can be used to meet a developed state's commitment under the Kyoto Protocol or traded on the international market for emission reduction units. The fact that the United States never became a party to the Kyoto Protocol and that emerging economies, such as China,

Brazil and India, were not subject to emission reduction obligations and could not obtain emission reduction units resulted in the protocol becoming increasingly controversial.

It is generally accepted that the Kyoto Protocol has not led to the desired reduction in GHG emissions. Efforts to negotiate a successor to the protocol have been ongoing since at least late 2007 but have proven difficult. In the meantime the 2012 Doha Amendment to the Kyoto Protocol was adopted. The amendment, which has not entered into force and might never enter into force, seeks to extend the Kyoto Protocol until 2020. States have also agreed that a new agreement should be in place by 2015 and in effect by 2020. Developments to date (September 2015) suggest that the new agreement, the Paris Agreement, will be built on so-called intended nationally determined contributions (INDCs) for all parties. INDCs will be submitted unilaterally by each participant in the regime and constitute a pledge to reduce GHG emissions. INDCs are to be transparent and will be subjected to a so-called measurement, reporting and verification (MRV) process. It also seems that the financial mechanism – funds that transfer financial means from developed to developing states parties – will be maintained and possibly expanded and that flexible mechanisms will continue to be part of the regime. In addition, it seems that mitigation and adaptation efforts will be more directly addressed by the new instrument.[14] This bottom-up approach to emission reduction commitments, instead of the top-down approach which characterized the Kyoto Protocol, thus seems to be the agreed way forward, even if many issues remain undecided and controversial, including the information that parties will have to submit regarding their INDCs and the content of the MRV process.

3.5 Addressing trade in hazardous substances

As discussed in section 2.2.1, trade measures, in the form of prohibitions to trade, are part of international regimes that seek to protect species of fauna and flora. The aim of these measures is to contribute to the protection of a species in its natural habitat. As illustrated above, trade measures also play a role in reducing operational pollution in the

---

14 A Negotiating text (full of square brackets, reflecting disagreement) for the successor of the Kyoto Protocol was agreed by the parties to the UNFCCC in February 2015, at a session of the Ad Hoc Working Group on the Durban Platform for Enhanced Action. This text is intended to provide the basis for a new agreement, to be adopted at COP 21, to be held in December 2015 in Paris.

form of bans to trade in hazardous substances, such as ozone-reducing substances (section 3.4.2). Trade in hazardous substances is also addressed by means of a particular decision-making procedure, known as the prior informed consent procedure. Regimes that include such a decision-making procedure are those regulating trade in hazardous waste,[15] hazardous chemicals and pesticides,[16] living modified organisms (LMOs)[17] and mercury.[18] Prior informed consent procedures tend to be expert-driven risk assessment procedures and questions about their appropriateness in regulating trade between developed and developing states have been raised. The regime regulating trade in hazardous waste has faced a particular problem related to a ban on the export of hazardous waste from developed to developing states, which illustrates how the North–South context may affect international environmental law. The same regime also provides an illustration of how different approaches to the treatment of decommissioned ships may compete in international environmental law, illustrating the fragmented nature of international environmental law. This section first addresses prior informed consent procedures. Thereafter it discusses the two aspects of the regime on trade in hazardous wastes mentioned above: the so-called "Ban Amendment" and the treatment of decommissioned ships.

3.5.1   Prior informed consent procedures

The prior informed consent procedures that are part of the four regimes referred to above entail that certain substances can only be exported with the prior informed written approval of the importing state. The Basel Convention subjects trade in hazardous wastes between its parties, including categories of wastes listed on its Annex I, wastes classified as hazardous by the importing states, and categories of wastes listed on its Annex II, to a prior informed consent procedure (Arts. 1, 4, 6). The Rotterdam Convention applies a prior informed consent procedure to those chemicals and pesticides listed in Annex III to the convention (Arts. 10, 11). The Cartagena Protocol applies the

---

15 1989 Basel Convention.
16 1998 Rotterdam Convention. The Rotterdam Convention was preceded by the 1985 Code of Conduct on the Distribution and Use of Pesticides adopted within Food and Agriculture Organization of the United Nations (FAO) and the 1987 UNEP London Guidelines for the Exchange of Information on Chemicals in International Trade, both instruments included a voluntary prior informed consent procedure.
17 2000 Cartagena Protocol.
18 Minamata Convention.

advanced informed agreement procedure, as the procedure is called in this instrument, to the import of LMOs intended for direct introduction into the environment, while a simplified procedure applies to LMOs intended for use in food, feed or for processing (Art. 7). The Minamata Convention applies the procedure to the export of mercury and its compounds (Art. 3(6)).

Prior informed consent procedures have been criticized because they involve complex risk assessments, which require sophisticated knowledge both in order to conduct them and in order to evaluate assessments conducted by others, often the exporters. It has been suggested that some developing states as a result of not having access to this knowledge cannot meaningfully participate in these procedures and thus are unable to provide their *informed* consent. Also noteworthy in this respect are the different ways in which the Basel Convention and the Cartagena Protocol, on the one hand, and the Rotterdam Convention, on the other hand, regulate the substances to which these procedures apply. The former allow importing states a measure of discretion: the Basel Convention by entitling a state of import to determine what it considers to be hazardous waste and prohibit its import (Art. 10(2), (4), (9)), the Cartagena Protocol by enabling the party of import to take a decision on each type of LMO intended for direct introduction into the environment (Arts. 7–10) and by not providing a list of materials that may be subjected to an import prohibition. The Rotterdam Convention operates by way of a different system. It determines that only substances listed on its Annex III can be subjected to the prior informed consent procedure; other chemicals must be allowed to access the market (Art. 7). The procedure for placing chemicals or pesticides on Annex III furthermore is a cumbersome one. In case of a hazardous chemical a proposal to place it on the list must be submitted by at least two states, which must come from different regions identified for purposes of the convention. The proposal is then subjected to expert review with the COP ultimately deciding by consensus whether the substance should be included in Annex III (Arts. 5, 7, 22). For pesticides the procedure is the same, except that a proposal to list a severely hazardous pesticide may be submitted by a single developing state (Arts. 6, 22). It is because of these rather tough procedures that the Rotterdam Convention has been characterized as an instrument that resists the international regulation of trade in hazardous chemicals and pesticides. Thus, the Rotterdam Convention, contrary to the reverse listing approach incorporated in the 1996 Protocol to the London Convention regarding dumping of waste at sea (section 3.4.2), does not automatically subject new hazardous chemicals or pesticides to its regulatory framework, that is its prior informed consent procedure.

3.5.2   Trade in hazardous waste and North–South relations

The Basel Convention was adopted in response to an increase in the export of hazardous wastes to Eastern European and developing states during the 1980s, exports that themselves were a reaction to the introduction of more stringent regulations for waste disposal and treatment in developed states. The Basel Convention seeks to limit the production of hazardous wastes, promote their environmentally sound treatment and prohibit the export of hazardous wastes unless sound environmental treatment is ensured (Art. 4). It prohibits the export of hazardous wastes to Antarctica (Art. 4(6)), to parties that ban the import of hazardous wastes (Art. 4(1)(b)) and to non-parties unless an agreement is in place that is no less environmentally sound than the convention (Arts. 4(5), 11). Where trade in hazardous wastes does take place it is governed by a regulatory system based on the prior informed consent procedure, discussed above.

The history of the Basel Convention is marked by the so-called "Ban Amendment" related to the export of hazardous wastes to developing states. Concerned by the export of hazardous wastes to developing states, in Africa in particular, African states adopted the 1991 Bamako Convention, which prohibits the import of hazardous wastes into Africa. In addition, they lobbied for an amendment to the Basel Convention that would prohibit the export of hazardous wastes to developing states. In 1994, their efforts resulted in the adoption of a COP decision prohibiting the transboundary movement of hazardous wastes destined for final disposal between OECD and non-OECD states and phasing out, by 31 December 1997, similar movements but destined for recovering or recycling. In 1995 this decision was transformed into an amendment to the Basel Convention. That amendment, however, has to date not entered into force.

The main reasons for the non-entry into force of the amendment, besides the fact that the parties to the convention are in disagreement about the applicable procedure, is that it imposes a complete ban on the export of hazardous wastes from developed to developing states. It thereby impedes developing states that have in place environmentally sound management processes for dealing with hazardous wastes from participating in the waste management industry. The history of the "Ban Amendment" illustrates the difficulty of on the one hand protecting states with a weak public sector, often developing states, and their populations from unethical waste traders while on the other hand enabling developing states and the private sector in these states, provided they meet certain standards, to profit from and participate in world trade.

3.5.3   Competing regulatory approaches to trade in decommissioned ships

Decommissioned ships are recycled because they contain valuable materials such as steel, which can be reused. However, they may also contain dangerous substances, such as asbestos. When ship recycling occurs in deficient facilities or on the beach, as is the case in some developing states, workers will be exposed to these dangerous substances and other hazardous conditions. It is these considerations which gave rise to the question whether ships destined for recycling are covered by the Basel Convention.

Article 2(1) of the Basel Convention defines "wastes" as "substances or objects which are disposed of or are intended to be disposed of or are required to be disposed of by the provisions of national law". Given the fact that a decommissioned ship as such will not be disposed of, doubts arose as to whether it was covered by the definition of "wastes", even if some of its components will be considered to be waste after the ship has been dismantled. However, in 2004 it was agreed that ships under certain conditions may become waste and would be covered by the Basel Convention. Yet, work on what would become the 2009 Hong Kong Convention continued under the auspices of the IMO.

The Hong Kong Convention regulates ship recycling by addressing both the state in which such activities take place and flag states. States in which ship recycling takes place are to apply the standards of the convention to these operations through a certification processes (Art. 4). Flag states are to ensure that ships meet the standards of the Hong Kong Convention, including provisions on prohibited materials and on the possession of an inventory of hazardous materials (Art. 4). The Hong Kong Convention thus is not based on a trade ban or a prior informed consent procedure but introduces a cradle to grave philosophy to the recycling of ships. This and other differences between the two regimes have resulted in disagreement between the parties to the Basel Convention about whether the Hong Kong Convention meets the "equivalent level of control" requirement established by Article 11 of the Basel Convention. Parties thus disagree as to whether the Hong Kong Convention may be applied *en lieu* of the Basel Convention or whether both conventions apply to the recycling of ships.

The situation discussed in this section illustrates the fragmented nature of international environmental law. It also points to how competing interests operate at the international level, with the shipping industry having a strong influence in the IMO, but less so in the forums associated with the Basel Convention.

3.6   Ecosystem-based governance

This section first traces how thinking about ecosystems, ecosystem-based governance and social-ecological relationships have evolved. It then illustrates how these conceptualizations, especially concerning the relationship between social and natural systems, are starting to affect governance arrangements.

3.6.1   Ecosystems, ecosystem governance and social-ecological resilience

The protected areas introduced by the 1933 Convention are the reflection of an early translation into international environmental law of the realization that in order to protect a species its habitat must also be protected (section 2.2.1). The designation of protected areas also signifies recognition of the interaction between various elements of an ecosystem, even if it might not have been expressed in these words at the time. The term "ecosystem", developed by Arthur Tansley in 1935,[19] refers to these interactions; it stresses the dynamics of these interactions and the interdependencies between living and non-living elements in natural systems. Ecology is the discipline that studies ecosystems. It identifies ecosystems at different scales and interactions among ecosystems.

An example of how dynamic interactions between ecosystems manifest themselves is the return of anchovy and sardines, during the 1990s, to the warmed waters of the North and Baltic Seas. This phenomenon

---

19 A.G. Tansley, "The Use and Abuse of Vegetational Concepts and Terms", 16(3) *Ecology* (1935) 284–307.

has been linked to oceanic and atmospheric dynamic interaction and ultimately climate change and the El Niño-Southern Oscillation, off the west coast of South America. The latter have also been linked to changing weather patterns and dengue activity in Australia. These dynamic interactions across the globe prompted James Lovelock, in 1979, to suggest that the Earth, as such, constitutes an ecosystem.[20] This idea finds reflection in paragraph 40 of "The Future We Want", the document adopted at the Rio+20 conference. It reads as follows:

> We call for holistic and integrated approaches to sustainable development that will guide *humanity to live in harmony with nature and lead to efforts to restore the health and integrity of the Earth's ecosystem.* (emphasis added)

Early ecosystem-based approaches focused on the management of the ecosystems as such and were usually referred to as ecosystem-based management approaches. More recently, it has been suggested that humans and their impact on the environment should be incorporated into ecosystem governance approaches as part of the system, leading to the characterization of those systems as social-ecological. Furthermore, it has been suggested that social-ecological systems should be managed so as to foster their resilience, thereby securing that the system is "safe to fail" for, fail it will. This approach entails that a social-ecological system should be governed so as to ensure that when it fails it will recover, instead of trying to manage a social-ecological system so that it is "fail safe", which is considered to be impossible. Social-ecological resilience research suggests that, while science is important for understanding relationships in social-ecological systems, factoring humans back into the system is paramount. Social-ecological resilience thinking stresses interdisciplinary and adaptive governance approaches which emphasize, among other things, social learning, the importance of diversity, integrative science, inclusive management and polycentric governance.[21] The complexities involved have also led to the suggestion that conventional scientific logic may not be well suited to deal with some of the issues at stake; instead fuzzy logic and heuristic approaches have been proposed as alternatives.

---

20 James Lovelock, *Gaia: A New Look at Life on Earth* (OUP, 1979).

21 Carl Folke, "Resilience: The Emergence of a Perspective for Social-Ecological Systems Analyses", *Global Environmental Change* 16 (2006) 253–67 (for an overview of the origins of social-ecological resilience thinking); Elinor Ostrom, "Polycentric Systems for Coping with Collective Action and Global Environmental Change", *Global Environmental Change* 20 (2010) 550–57 (on polycentric governance).

Ideas about social-ecological resilience provide a challenge to international environmental law, since it has been developed in a rather slow and piecemeal fashion and is not renowned for its adaptive capacity. An example is the principle of the freedom of fishing, advocated by Grotius in the early seventeenth century, which has been instrumental in facilitating overfishing. Similarly, the concept of maximum sustainable yield (MSY), developed during the mid-twentieth century and intended to limit fishing activities, received significant criticism as of the 1970s. Yet, both the freedom of fishing and MSY continue to be part of international fisheries law (section 5.2.3), even if the 1995 Fish Stocks Agreement has now supplemented these notions with a management system based on precautionary reference points (section 4.6.2).

The 2005 Millennium Ecosystem Assessment (MA) clearly pronounced itself on the dire state of ecosystems and links this state to human actions. The UNEP-based website for the MA summarizes its main findings as follows:

> The bottom line of the MA findings is that human actions are depleting Earth's natural capital, putting such strain on the environment that the ability of the planet's ecosystems to sustain future generations can no longer be taken for granted. At the same time, the assessment shows that with appropriate actions it is possible to reverse the degradation of many ecosystem services over the next 50 years, but the changes in policy and practice required are substantial and not currently underway.

Note that the concern in the above-quoted paragraph is with reversing the degradation of ecosystem services, not ecosystems. This approach reflects an anthropocentric approach to the environment since it is the services that ecosystems offer humans that we are interested in, not the ecosystems themselves (section 1.2.1). The term "ecosystem services", moreover, is controversial because it is also used in economic literature to assess the monetary value of ecosystems and the services they provide to humans. This economic conceptualization of ecosystems is criticized based on the argument that ecosystems represent values that extend beyond the monetary.

3.6.2   Ecosystems and governance arrangements

Ecosystem-based governance approaches have been incorporated into international environmental law, even if often in a piecemeal fashion.

Traces of social-ecological resilience thinking have emerged only recently in international environmental law.

An early example of an instrument that explicitly recognizes that it is human activities that need to be managed and integrated into relevant policies and that also refers to the need to incorporate uncertainty into decision-making by way of adaptive management and regular review of policy is the 2007 Baltic Sea Action Plan adopted within the framework of the 1992 Helsinki Convention.[22] Its Preamble provides, among other things, that:

> STRESSING the need for integrated management of human activities and the need to take into account their impacts on the marine environment in all policies and programmes implemented in the Baltic Sea region . . .

> ACKNOWLEDGING that the current environmental as well as reduction targets in the various segments are based on best available knowledge of today. Pursuing the adaptive management principles, the objectives and targets should be periodically reviewed and revised using a harmonised approach and most updated information . . .

The Biodiversity Convention, with in situ conservation as its preferred mode of conservation, in principle relates positively to ecosystem-based governance approaches (Art. 8) (section 2.2.1). However, the 2000 COP Decision V/6, entitled "Ecosystem Approach", illustrates considerable doubt as to how to move forward, especially if considered in terms of social-ecological resilience thinking. On the one hand, the decision explicitly adopts an ecosystem-based management approach which is describes as ". . . a strategy for the integrated management of land, water and living resources that promotes conservation and sustainable use in an equitable way" (para. A.1). The decision furthermore embraces adaptive management and a learning-by-doing approach (para. A.4) and recognizes that decentralized management and stakeholder participation are important elements in ecosystem management (Principle 2). On the other hand, the decision maintains that "humans . . . are an integral component of *many* eco-systems" (emphasis added, para. A.2) and that more or less all management and conservation approaches are compatible with an ecosystem-based approach (para. A.5). The latter elements of the decision are not so much shortcomings but rather point to the difficulty of identifying the

---

22 The Helsinki Convention was preceded by a 1974 treaty of the same name.

ways in which to develop ecosystem-based governance approaches. In 2004 the COP further developed the ecosystem-based approach and, for example, recognized that sustainable forest management strategies developed within the ambit of the Statement on Forests, integrated-river basin management, integrated marine and coastal area management and responsible fisheries approaches may be consistent with ecosystem-based approaches (paras. 7, 8, Decision VII/11). Moreover, it recognized the relevance of public participation in all phases of decision-making and of monitoring and review and good governance (paras. 14, 17, 18, Decision VII/11). Even if in rather general terms, the ecosystem-based approach developed by the COP thus recognizes that governance structures matter.

The 2010 Strategic Plan for Biodiversity 2011–2020, a period that coincides with the United Nations Decade on Biodiversity, underscores the difficulty of identifying how we might move forward on developing ecosystem-based governance structures (Annex to Decision X/2). Its paragraph 3 provides that "[b]iological diversity underpins ecosystem functioning and the provision of ecosystem services for human well-being". This quote suggests that it is the ecosystem services that we are interested in and that it is biological diversity and ecosystems that need to be protected in order to secure those services. The plan thereby conceptualizes one side of the equation, the importance of ecosystems for humans. It also hesitantly starts to conceptualize how humans, including our social systems, interact with ecosystems and the type of governance structure that might foster biodiversity and ecosystem protection. The hesitancy in the document can probably be attributed to the fact that it is at this juncture that fundamental differences of opinion are encountered, for example about which subsidies are harmful for biodiversity and ecosystems. Target 3 of the plan underscores this point. It provides that states shall ensure that "[b]y 2020, at the latest, incentives, including subsidies, harmful to biodiversity are eliminated, phased out or reformed in order to minimize or avoid negative impacts". It thus seems to be agreed that some subsidies might have negative effects on the preservation of biological diversity and ecosystems, but not which subsidies might fit this category. It might also be argued that decisions about subsidies should be taken at more local levels of decision-making and that Target 3 aims to foster the debate at those more local levels.

The Ecosystem Approach to Fisheries (EAF), introduced by the Food and Agriculture Organization of the United Nations (FAO) in 2003 might provide some insight on how to proceed. The EAF in 2009 conceptualized a "fishery system" as "a social-ecological system, and consists of linkages between people and the environment, also outside the actual fishing operations".[23] The FAO also emphasizes that the EAF is an iterative and adaptive management process, which is never perfect, and which should be participatory. The EAF thereby introduces social-ecological resilience thinking into fisheries policy. It also provides a rationale for, among other things, restricting subsidies to the fisheries sector, introducing MPAs (section 2.2.1) and regulating trade in endangered species of fish. The latter has been a bone of contention between CITES and fisheries conservation bodies, with the former arguing that endangered species of fish qualify for listing on the CITES lists, while the latter argue that conservation of fisheries resources is solely in their purview.

3.7   The Anthropocene

The quotation from paragraph 40 of "The Future We Want" (section 3.6) in referring to "the integrity of the Earth's ecosystem" reflects a concern that has been identified relatively recently. It relates to the finding that since the advent of the Industrial Revolution, in roughly 1750, human activity has been impacting the Earth's systems. It has been suggested that as a result the Earth has entered a new geological epoch: the Anthropocene. In this epoch humans are affecting the Earth's systems in ways similar to natural phenomena, such as meteorites, which when they collided with the Earth have caused the extinction of species.

Climate change and ozone layer depletion are developments that clearly point in this direction, even if the ozone layer might recover (section 3.4.2). Ocean acidification, linked to climate change, points in the same direction and provides an example of the dynamics involved in natural systems. Ocean acidification is caused when CO_2 dissolves in ocean waters, increasing its acidity. Acidic marine waters, among other things, result in the destruction of coral reefs and a lack of or deficient shell production in both naturally and commercially growing marine species. Acidification of ocean waters affects individual specimens, species, the food chain and ultimately marine ecosystems. Other examples of how human activity may be affecting planetary boundaries

---

23 FAO, Technical Guidelines for Responsible Fisheries, 4, Supp. 2 Add. 2, (2009) p. 15.

include biodiversity loss and disturbance of the Earth's nitrogen cycle. Together these incursions on planetary boundaries suggest that we may indeed be living in the Anthropocene, where human activities are a driving force for changes in the Earth's systems. International environmental law clearly has not come to terms with these findings The successor to the Kyoto Protocol, planned for adoption in December 2015, will provide an opportunity to ascertain to what extent the realization that we are living in the Anthropocene will resound in international environmental law.

3.8 Assessment

The insights about what should be addressed by international environmental law clearly show increased complexity over time. From keeping polluting substances out of the environment by addressing both accidental and operational pollution, to addressing trade in hazardous substances and introducing ecosystem-based governance approaches. These complexities, together with those addressed in the previous chapter, merit the qualification of environmental problems as social-ecological problems, where the economic is subsumed into the social. The insight that we are living in the Anthropocene further complicates the task international environmental law will have to live up to.

Scientific knowledge and technology will play an important role in addressing social-ecological problems. However, increasingly the focus will need to be on human conduct and how humans relate to their environment and to each other when they take elements from the environment or when they engage in trade. The EAF, introduced by the FAO, offers an example of the types of approaches that may be required, even if the resulting local fisheries management plans will never be perfected and require constant work. This realization points to another insight which seems to be emerging: while the challenges we face are daunting and global in nature, concrete solutions will have to be found at local levels by way of iterative, adaptive and participatory decision-making processes. What then might the role of international environmental law be? Might it be the fostering of polycentric governance in which local participatory decision-making processes are linked to national, regional and international participatory decision-making processes and in which the focus is on what constitutes good governance?

The next three chapters illustrate how international environmental law at the level of principles, institutional structure and dispute settlement and accountability procedures seeks to address some of the daunting questions raised above.

4 Principles

4.1 Introduction

In international environmental law principles serve to frame legal debate, guide negotiations and the interpretation and application of treaties, customary international law as well as regimes developed by private actors. This chapter considers the most important principles that play a role in international environmental law. It starts with a section on documents that have been developed over time and that provide overviews of relevant principles, followed by a section on the legal status of principles of international environmental law. Thereafter, the most important principles will be considered. The principle of cooperation will be discussed first since it permeates international environmental law and points to the varied and complex relations of interdependence that inform international environmental law (section 4.4). Principles that translate those relations of interdependence into legally relevant relations will be considered next (section 4.5). Thereafter principles that determine the diligence that may be expected of states (section 4.6) and operational principles (section 4.7) will be discussed, that is principles that, respectively indicate *when* action is to be taken and *how* things are to be done, given complex relations of interdependence.

4.2 Relevant documents

Principles that play a role in international environmental law have been set out systematically in a number of documents adopted at the global level, besides having been incorporated into treaties. The most prominent among these global documents is the 1992 Rio Declaration. The Rio Declaration, however, is heavily indebted to the 1972 Stockholm Declaration on which it builds. Other documents that have played and continue to play a role in the development of relevant principles are the following. The 1982 World Charter for Nature, adopted by UNGA

(UNGA Res. 37/7(1982)); the 1987 Proposed Legal Principles for Environmental Protection and Sustainable Development, developed by the WCED Experts Group on Environmental Law (WCED Principles); the 1995 IUCN Draft International Covenant on Environment and Development (IUCN Draft Covenant), last revised in 2010; and the International Law Association's (ILA) 2002 New Delhi Declaration of Principles of International Law Relating to Sustainable Development (ILA Declaration).

The above-mentioned documents illustrate a number of developments. First, their titles, as the titles of successive summits (section 2.3), point to the shift of focus from protection of the environment to attaining sustainable development. Second, their contents illustrate that attaining sustainable development is increasingly perceived as a question of good governance (section 3.6). Third, they illustrate the dynamic interaction between NGOs, such as IUCN and the ILA, and inter-state bodies. Noteworthy in this respect is that the first draft of the World Charter for Nature was prepared by IUCN, in 1979, and that the ILA Declaration was submitted to the United Nations by Bangladesh and the Netherlands for circulation as an official United Nations document for the World Summit on Sustainable Development (UN Doc. A/Conf. 199/8 (2002)). Fourth, while the development of international environmental law played a prominent role in the preparation and outcomes of earlier summits (Stockholm and Rio), this has not been the case for more recent summits (World Summit on Sustainable Development and Rio+20).

This chapter uses principles as formulated in the Rio Declaration as reference points. This choice was made because the Declaration and its content garnered the overall approval of states in 1992 and because states reaffirmed that support at the World Summit on Sustainable Development and Rio+20 (para. 8, Johannesburg Declaration and para. 15 "The Future We Want"). In addition, many of the Rio Principles were foreshadowed in the Stockholm Declaration. The fact that the Rio Principles can count on the overall support of states means that they are authoritative, but also that they reflect significant compromise.

4.3 Legal status

The legal status of principles that play a role in international environmental law, as of principles that figure in international law, is the subject of thriving debate. This debate as such will not be engaged in here, even if a few general remarks about the legal status of principles in international environmental law are in order.

First, the documents mentioned above, including the Rio Declaration, as such are not legally binding. However, their content, that is individual principles, may become part of international law, as general principles of international law or customary international law. The most authoritative evidence of a principle attaining this status is if a court or tribunal recognizes the relevant principle as part of international law (section 4.5.2). Indications about the legal status of a principle may also be found in national law and in decisions taken by and documents emanating from states, international organizations and other relevant actors.

Second, relevant principles have been incorporated into treaties, explicitly and more often implicitly, in these cases they are part of treaty law. An example of an explicit but ambiguous reference to a principle is contained in Article 5(c) of the Fish Stocks Agreement. It provides that the precautionary approach is among the general principles that are to guide the parties in implementing the agreement (section 4.6.2). An example of an implicit reference to a principle is Article 20 of the Biodiversity Convention. It implicitly incorporates the principle of common but differentiated responsibilities by committing developed states to make available financial resources to developing states and making the implementation of the convention by developing states conditional on the extent to which developed states meet this commitment and their commitment to transfer technology (section 4.5.7).

Third, international courts and tribunals are rather careful when they have the opportunity to express themselves on the legal status of international environmental law principles. On some occasions they have explicitly declared a principle to have legally binding status; however, when in doubt courts and tribunals leave the legal status undecided. The considerations by the tribunal in the 2005 *Iron Rhine* arbitration between Belgium and the Netherlands provide an example. When discussing the question which environmental treaties or principles have contributed to the development of customary international law it observed that:

in all of these categories "environment" is broadly referred to as including air, water, land, flora and fauna, natural ecosystems and sites, human health and safety, and climate. The emerging principles, *whatever their current status*, make reference to conservation, management, notions of prevention and of sustainable development, and protection for future generations. (para. 58, emphasis added)

The tribunal, however, also held that as a "principle of general international law" "where development may cause significant harm to the environment there is a duty to prevent, or at least mitigate, such harm" (para. 59).

The cautious attitude of courts and tribunals can be explained by the compromise reflected in the formulation of many principles that play a role in international environmental law as well as by the manner in which they have been incorporated into treaties. Article 5(c) of the Fish Stocks Agreement, referred to above, provides an example. The chapeau of the Article refers to "general principles", while Article 5(c) and other provisions of the agreement refer to the "precautionary approach". Is this an incorporation of the precautionary principle or the precautionary approach? And what is the difference? One might argue that referring to something as a principle in a legal text makes it a principle of law, while referring to something as an approach makes it part of policy. Alternatively, it might be argued that Article 5(c) of the Fish Stocks Agreement as a matter of legal principle requires that fisheries policies for straddling and migratory stocks adopt a precautionary approach.

4.4 Cooperation

In theory preventing disturbances and pollutants from harming the environment does not require states to cooperate; in an ideal world it could be attained by individual states taking measures to prevent such disturbances and pollution. However, in practice cooperation makes sense. First, cooperation makes sense because states that share a resource may interfere with each other's uses. An international river with several riparian states provides an example. In this case upstream pollution may restrict down-stream states in their use of the water. Second, cooperation avoids that measures taken in one state are annulled by the lack of or different measures taken in another state. For example, on a lake shared by two states if one state decides to limit the input of harmful substance A and the other state decides not to, the environment will still have to endure substance A and the effect of the first state's regulation might be negligible. Similarly, if states share a fish stock which is in danger of being depleted, it will be of little avail to the stock if one state limits its fishing capacity and the other states continue to allow new entrants into the fishery. Third, cooperation makes sense because it levels the playing field for private sector actors by ensuring that similar measures apply to comparable activities. Such measures entail, for example, that plants employing comparable production processes would be subject to the same BAT standards, and thus incur comparable costs. As our economies have become more interdependent the rationale for levelling the playing field extends over larger geographic areas, as exemplified by disputes at the WTO over, for example, food safety standards and subsidies to energy-producing plants (sections 7.4.3, 7.4.5). Fourth, as a result of international trade localities across the globe have become interdependent, requiring cooperation. Think of the subsistence farmer who loses her livelihood after having been displaced from her land because a foreign company has been given a licence to engage in a large-scale commercial agricultural activity for export purposes (section 2.4); of Nile Perch caught especially for the export market (section 3.2); CDM projects and trade in the CERs that they generate (section 3.4.3); or trade in decommissioned ships (section 3.5.3). Finally, and importantly, cooperation makes sense because we have come to realize that the Earth's environment is characterized by relations of interdependence on which all of us depend and which may be affected by human activities taking place anywhere on Earth (sections 3.6, 3.7). It is these considerations that place the principle of cooperation at the centre of contemporary international environmental law.

Principle 27 of the Rio Declaration formulates the cooperation principle as follows:

> States and people shall cooperate in good faith and in a spirit of partnership in the fulfilment of the principles embodied in this Declaration and in the further development of international law in the field of sustainable development.

Note that Principle 27 refers to both "states" and "people"; it thereby extends the duty to cooperate to individuals and groups in society. The Rio Declaration also refers to the duty to cooperate for states and people in relation to the eradication of poverty (Principle 5). Furthermore, it requires states to cooperate in relation to the protection of the Earth's ecosystem (Principle 7); to improve endogenous capacity for sustainable development (Principle 9); and to avoid the relocation and transfer to other states of activities or substances that may harm the environment (Principle 14). The Rio Declaration, moreover, foresees an important role for partnerships between states and other actors. The latter is evidenced by Principles 20–22 of the Rio Declaration on the importance of involving women, youth and indigenous and local communities in furthering sustainable development.

In hindsight, the absence of a specific reference to the private sector in the Rio Declaration, and in the WCED Principles, is remarkable. The private sector drew attention especially at the World Summit on Sustainable Development, which called for the promotion of public-private partnerships, especially in its Plan of Implementation. The Johannesburg Declaration refers to the duty of the private sector "to contribute to the evolution of equitable and sustainable communities and societies" (para. 27) and to the need of the private sector to "enforce corporate accountability" (para. 29). The IUCN Draft Covenant also focuses mainly on public actors, referring to the private sector as having a responsibility to take measures to eradicate poverty (Art. 31) and as a source of financial means to realize sustainable development (Arts. 51, 52). The ILA Declaration takes a broader perspective. It suggests that corporations, in particular transnational corporations, "should" (not shall) contribute to attaining sustainable development and have responsibilities with regard to the polluter pays principle (para. 3.1). It also commits the business community to the precautionary approach (para. 4.1) and asserts that good governance "calls for corporate social responsibility and socially responsible investments as conditions for the existence of a global market aimed at a fair distribution of wealth among and within communities" (para. 6.3). The ILA Declaration thereby addresses transnational corporations and their relationship to human rights and thus situations such as those in Bhopal, India, in Ogoniland, Nigeria, and in Ecuador, (sections 3.3.3, 6.4.3, 7.2.2, 7.5). The IUCN Draft Covenant also addresses transnational corporations, but does so indirectly, in terms of the responsibility of the home state (Art. 35). International environmental law thus to some extent recognizes that private sector actors may have a significant impact on the environment in states other than their home state but remains reluctant to address them directly.

4.5   Relations of interdependence

International environmental law, like all international law or all law, can be characterized as dealing with relations of interdependence and many of its principles serve to translate factual relations of interdependence into legally relevant relationships. In other words, these principles suggest that because states, and in some cases also other actors, are interdependent in certain ways they should act accordingly. For example, states are interdependent because air streams cross their boundaries therefore they should act so as to prevent transboundary harm by way of air pollution. While early principles, such as the no harm rule, focused on physical interdependence grounded in the environment itself, more recently developed principles consider more complex relations of interdependence both in terms of space and over time. Examples are the principle of intra-generational equity and the principle of inter-generational equity. The former addresses relationships of interdependence within a generation and relates to, in particular, issues of distributive justice across the globe; the latter addresses relationships between generations and stretches across time. Principles that address relationships of interdependence are discussed in this section.

4.5.1   No harm

One of the earliest principles to emerge in international environmental law is the duty to prevent transboundary harm, or the no harm principle. It was applied in the 1941 *Trail Smelter* arbitration (section 2.3) and is linked to a more general duty of care that states owe each other. The latter was espoused by the International Court of Justice (ICJ) in the 1949 *Corfu Channel* case. In this case the Court held that it is "... every State's obligation not to allow knowingly its territory to be used for acts contrary to the rights of other States . . ." (p. 22). The no harm principle has evolved to include every state's duty to prevent environmental harm to areas beyond national jurisdiction, that is, the high seas, Antarctica and outer space. The duty to prevent transboundary environmental harm and harm to areas beyond national jurisdiction was formulated in Principle 21 of the Stockholm Declaration. Principle 2 of the Rio Declaration conveys it as follows:

> States have, in accordance with the Charter of the United Nations and the principles of international law, the sovereign right to exploit their own resources pursuant to their own environmental and developmental policies,

and *the responsibility to ensure that activities within their jurisdiction or control do not cause damage to the environment of other States or of areas beyond the limits of national jurisdiction.* (emphasis added)

The ICJ in its 1996 advisory opinion on *Nuclear Weapons* declared the principle to be part of international law when it held that:

> The existence of the general obligation of States to ensure that activities within their jurisdiction and control respect the environment of other States or of areas beyond national control is now part of the corpus of international law relating to the environment. (para. 29)

Note that the ICJ here is referring to a transboundary situation whereas the tribunal in the *Iron Rhine* arbitration, quoted in section 4.3, formulated the duty to prevent harm to the environment more generally. The tribunal thereby held that the no harm principle also applies to a situation in which states were engaged in a cooperative project, redeveloping the portion of transboundary railroad track, located in the territory of one of the two states.

Principle 2 of the Rio Declaration also refers to the "sovereign right [of states] to exploit their own resources". This terminology is closely linked to the doctrine of state sovereignty and to the concept of "permanent sovereignty over natural resources", which emerged from the efforts of developing states to establish a NIEO during the 1970s (section 2.4). It also points to a tension that plays a prominent role in international (environmental) law as we increasingly become aware of interdependencies: finding a balance between state sovereignty on the one hand and the need for cooperation, and thus limiting state sovereignty, on the other hand. This tension is particularly evident in regimes which require states to restrict their sovereignty in the common interest, or the interest of the international community, without transboundary effects literally arising. The Biodiversity Convention, discussed in the following two sections, provides an example of such a regime.

4.5.2 Equitable and reasonable utilization

MEAs may require states to ensure equitable and reasonable, sustainable or wise use of the environment, its components or ecosystems. Relevant examples are the Biodiversity Convention, which refers to the sustainable use of components of biodiversity (Art. 10) and the Ramsar Convention, which propagates the wise use of wetlands (Art.

3(1)). These MEAs require states to implement these principles in their national legislation for purposes of ensuring the sustainable or wise use of the resources within their territory or jurisdiction. In other words, these regimes do not explicitly prescribe these principles for transboundary situations. In transboundary situations the no harm principle would apply, unless states in an agreement in relation to a specific transboundary ecosystem or a specific type of transboundary ecosystem have agreed otherwise. The Great Lakes Agreement provides an example of an agreement for a specific transboundary ecosystem, the Great Lakes in North America. It sets certain objectives, including that the Great Lakes shall be free from invasive species that would adversely impact water quality (Art. 3(1)(a)(vii)). The agreement thereby implies that the introduction of invasive species would compromise the due diligence (section 4.6) that the parties to the agreement owe each other, and as a result moves beyond the no harm principle.

The 1997 Watercourses Convention is an example of an agreement that goes beyond the no harm principle for international watercourses in general. It requires watercourse states to "in their respective territories utilize an international watercourse in an equitable and reasonable manner" with the aim of "attaining optimal and sustainable utilization" of the watercourse and requires them to cooperate towards that end (Art. 5). The Convention also determines that in attaining equitable and reasonable use all relevant factors shall be taken into account, including natural, social and economic factors and existing and future uses and their effects (Art. 6). The Watercourses Convention, then, does not only require cooperation but also sets a goal for that cooperation – optimal and sustainable utilization – and specifies how that goal is to be attained – by ensuring equitable and reasonable use. The Convention thereby moves beyond the no harm rule, codified in its Article 7.

The approach embodied in the Watercourses Convention probably explains why many states have been reluctant to become a party to it. The list of states parties reveals that many states with considerable interests in international watercourses are not parties to the Convention. Such states include Egypt, Ethiopia and Sudan, which are among the riparian states of the Nile, and Canada, Mexico and the United States, which share various international watercourses that cross respectively the Canadian–United States and Mexican–United States border. What deters these states from becoming a party to the

Watercourses Convention? It might well be that they consider the Watercourses Convention to have too big an effect on their sovereignty by moving beyond the no harm principle, contained in its Article 7, by including the principle of equitable and reasonable utilization in Article 5. The Watercourses Convention based on Article 5, in principle, sanctions the argument by state A that an activity involving a use of the watercourse by state B is not equitable and reasonable because the interests of state A in the same watercourse have not been taken into account. Based on the 1975 River Uruguay Statute, concluded between Argentina and Uruguay, the ICJ sanctioned exactly this argument in its 2010 judgment in *Pulp Mills* when it held that:

> such utilization could not be considered to be equitable and reasonable if the interests of the other riparian State in the shared resource and the environmental protection of the latter were not taken into account. (para. 177)

It added that a provision in the Statute, requiring consultation about water uses of the transboundary Uruguay River:

> embodies this interconnectedness between equitable and reasonable utilization of a shared resource and the balance between economic development and environmental protection that is the essence of sustainable development. (para. 177)

The Court thereby established a link between the interests of riparian states in the utilization of an international watercourse and the broader interests reflected in the concept of sustainable development (section 4.5.4). The Court in this case, as it had in the case concerning the 1997 *Gabčíkovo-Nagymaros* project, between Hungary and Slovakia, read contemporary principles of international environmental and water law – sustainable development and equitable and reasonable utilization – into a treaty, the River Uruguay Statute, which does not refer to these principles. In *Gabčíkovo-Nagymaros* the ICJ found that general provisions requiring the protection of the environment, what the Court referred to as "evolving provisions", contained in a 1970 treaty concluded between Czechoslovakia and Hungary, necessitated the incorporation of newly developed norms of international environmental law into the regime. It held that:

> By inserting these evolving provisions in the Treaty, the parties recognized the potential necessity to adapt the Project. Consequently, the Treaty is

not static, and is open to adapt to emerging norms of international law. By means of Articles 15 and 19, new environmental norms can be incorporated in the Joint Contractual Plan. (para. 112)

The Court furthermore concluded that incorporating such new norms into the project was a joint responsibility of Hungary and Slovakia which required "a mutual willingness to discuss in good faith actual and potential environmental risks" and required the continuous assessment of environmental risks (para. 112). The Court thereby did not only require the states concerned to cooperate but to cooperate in a certain way. Namely, they are to engage in the continuous assessment of actual and potential environmental harm (section 4.7.4).

Based on the rulings of the ICJ in *Gabčíkovo-Nagymaros* and *Pulp Mills* the conclusion can be drawn that general international environmental law will co-determine the concrete obligations that arise for states parties to a treaty that contains a provision requiring cooperation to protect the environment or consultations about uses of a resource. Furthermore, the ruling in *Pulp Mills* suggests that for international watercourses, the principle of equitable and reasonable utilization has attained customary international law status or at least is relevant beyond the parties to the Watercourses Convention, since neither Argentina nor Uruguay are parties to this convention. International environmental law thus, at least for international watercourses, has moved beyond the no harm rule (section 4.5.1) to include the principle of equitable and reasonable utilization.

4.5.3   Common concern of humankind

Contemporary international environmental law has also moved beyond the no harm rule contained in Principle 2 of the Rio Declaration by incorporating a focus on issues that are "of common concern", thereby expanding relations of interdependence beyond those of neighbouring states. The IUCN Draft Covenant and the ILA Declaration refer to, respectively, "the global environment" (Art. 3) and "the protection, preservation and enhancement of the natural environment, particularly the proper management of climate system, biological diversity and fauna and flora of the Earth" (Art. 1.3) as of common concern to humankind. The ILA Declaration in its preamble also refers to sustainable development as "a matter of common concern". Moreover, the "conservation of biological diversity" and "the change in the Earth's climate and its adverse effects" have been declared the common concern of humankind, in the preambles of, respectively, the Biodiversity Convention and the UNFCCC.

In case of the conservation of biological diversity the following is at stake. We all potentially profit from the conservation of biological diversity anywhere in the world, for example by medicine developed from plants in the tropical rainforest or because forests function as the "lungs" of the Earth and contribute to the reduction of CO_2. The rationale for cooperation in the case of the conservation of biological diversity thus involves both the prevention of harm and the sharing of benefits that biological diversity provides. Problematic in this respect is the fact that remaining areas with an abundance of biodiversity are found mainly in the South, thus leading to pressure on developing states to conserve their environment in the interest not only of their own population, but in the interest of the Earth's population as a whole. In the case of the climate system the rationale involves the following. Greenhouse gases emitted anywhere will affect the Earth's climate system with the consequences thereof potentially materializing anywhere on Earth.

The principle of the common concern of humankind needs to be distinguished from the principle of the common heritage of mankind, which applies to the "Area", in other words, the seabed and ocean floor and subsoil thereof beyond the limits of national jurisdiction, and its resources (Art. 136 juncto Art. 1(1), LOS Convention). The principle of the common heritage of mankind thus refers to the legal status of the Area and its resources as such, excluding them from the jurisdiction of states and bringing them under "international jurisdiction". The principle of common concern of humankind, instead, leaves the legal status of the locality and the resources in that locality intact, even if it provides other states with a basis for submitting that they have an interest in the resource in question and thus its protection.

Even if framed in terms of Japan having violated its obligations under the 1946 International Whaling Convention, the Australian claim considered by the ICJ in its 2014 decision in *Whaling in the Antarctic*, might be regarded as involving a common concern, or at least a common concern of the parties to the Whaling Convention. That is, the common concern in the conservation of whales and thus proper implementation of the moratorium on whaling and the exception thereto for scientific whaling, based on which Japan was engaged in whaling (Art. 8). However, had Australia brought its claim before the

Court in those terms, it would probably not have succeeded, given that it remains controversial whether a breach of the common concern is as such justiciable under international law. This is the case even if the 2007 Articles on State Responsibility, adopted by the UNGA (UNGA Res. 62/6), recognize that a state, as an injured state or as a non-injured state, may under certain conditions invoke the responsibility of another state arising from obligations owed to the international community or to a group of states (Arts. 42, 48). These provisions, however, are controversial and their customary international law status is the subject of debate.

The plastics that circulate the world oceans arguably present a new common concern (section 3.2). International environmental law does not currently provide a regulatory regime that addresses their removal, even if regional seas conventions are starting to address the problem of plastics entering the marine environment (section 5.2.4). Viable means of removing the plastics do not seem to be available yet and any removal options are likely to be technically demanding and costly. At present, the subject is being studied by the Joint Group of Experts on the Scientific Aspects of Marine Environmental Protection (GESAMP). GESAMP was established in 1968 by the IMO, the FAO, the International Intergovernmental Oceanographic Commission of the United Nations Educational, Scientific and Cultural Organization's (UNESCO) and the World Meteorological Organization (WMO). It is currently sponsored by nine international organizations, which have responsibilities related to the marine environment, including the United Nations. The current situation regarding plastics circulating the oceans illustrates the danger of relying on the carrying capacity of the environment (section 3.2) and in hindsight the relevance of the principles of prevention and precaution (section 4.6). It also shows that when faced with an environmental problem that arguably is of common concern and involves considerable uncertainties states implement their shared responsibility and the duty to cooperate by investing in collaborative scientific research. A similar approach was adopted when human-induced climate change was still an issue of debate. At the time, in 1988, the Intergovernmental Panel on Climate Change (IPCC) was established with the aim of investigating the causes of climate change. Lastly, the plastics problem also shows interconnections across the globe and that what we decide to do with our plastics at the most local of levels matters.

4.5.4   Sustainable development

Sustainable development entered mainstream international environmental law via *Our Common Future*, the report of the WCED, published in 1990 (section 2.3), even if it was foreshadowed in the Stockholm Declaration (Principles 8, 9). The report describes sustainable development as ". . . development that meets the needs of the present without compromising the ability of future generations to meet their own needs" (p. 43).

Sustainable development is probably best regarded as a concept or objective that aims to integrate developmental and environmental concerns. It is often portrayed as consisting of three intimately related pillars: social, economic and environmental, which need to be considered simultaneously. This integrative role of the concept of sustainable development was emphasized by the ICJ in its decision in *Gabčíkovo-Nagymaros*, even if it referred to only two dimensions of the concept. The ICJ found that the "need to reconcile economic development with protection of the environment is aptly expressed in the concept of sustainable development" (para. 140).

While the Rio Declaration does not itself define sustainable development, its Principles 3 and 4 contain what comes closest to indicating what the principle means:

Principle 3
The right to development must be fulfilled so as to equitably meet developmental and environmental needs of present and future generations.

Principle 4
In order to achieve sustainable development, environmental protection shall constitute an integral part of the development process and cannot be considered in isolation from it.

Based on these Rio Principles it might be argued that the Rio Declaration, by emphasizing the need to integrate environmental concerns into the development process, prioritizes development, even if many of its principles also focus on environmental protection. The IUCN Draft Covenant adopts a different approach to sustainable development. Article 1 of the IUCN Draft Covenant provides that the aim of the covenant is "achieving environmental conservation, an indispensable foundation for sustainable development". It thereby prioritizes environmental conservation. This is not to say that the IUCN Draft Covenant rejects the importance of development. On the contrary, it, for example, provides that "peace, development, environmental conservation and respect for human rights and fundamental freedoms are indivisible, interrelated and interdependent, and constitute the foundation of a sustainable world" (Art. 4) and includes the right to development (Art. 10) and the need to eradicate poverty (Arts. 11, 31). The ILA Declaration, as is evidenced by its title, takes sustainable development as its point of departure but adopts an integrated approach to the topic.

The different approaches identified above point to a tension which already manifested itself during the preparations for the 1972 Stockholm Conference (section 2.4). It involves the following questions. Should our primary concern be the protection of the environment and will that serve development, including the eradication of poverty? Or, should our primary concern be development, including the eradication of poverty, and will that serve the environment? It is this tension that the concept of sustainable development seeks to breach by suggesting that development and environmental protection factually are intimately related and normatively should be integrated.

The Rio Declaration in Principle 3, quoted above, and in Principle 7 (section 4.5.7) provide an indication of the types of considerations that should play a role in implementing sustainable development by formulating, in particular, the principles of inter-generational equity, intra-generational equity and common but differentiated responsibilities. These principles were foreshadowed by the Stockholm Declaration and also resound in the other documents referred to in the introduction of this chapter, especially those adopted after the Rio Declaration.

4.5.5   Inter-generational equity

The principle of inter-generational equity refers to equity between generations. It means that the interests of future generations, in particular in a sustained resource base and a healthy environment, should be taken into account when the present generation determines its environmental and developmental policies. The main thrust of the principle is that our actions today should not limit the choices that future generations have available to them. Inter-generational equity, then, requires the present generation to take into account the long-term effects of its activities such as the difficulties encountered and timelines involved in restoring disturbed ecosystems. As formulated in Principle 3 of the Rio Declaration, inter-generational equity is closely related to the right to development, which as such remains contested under international law.

While most environmental agreements aim at the long-term preservation of the environment and its resources and might thus be said to foster inter-generational equity, some treaties, especially more recent ones, explicitly refer to the interests of future generations. An early convention that refers to future generations is the 1946 International Whaling Convention, even if it presents that interest as pertaining to "nations" (preamble). A more recent example is the Biodiversity Convention, which in its preamble provides that biological diversity is to be conserved and used sustainably "for the benefit of present and future generations".

One of the difficulties encountered in implementing the principle of inter-generational equity is the fact that future generations are unable to voice their own interests, are not "represented at the table". A landmark case that recognized the principle of inter-generational equity is the 1993 decision of the Philippine Supreme Court in *Minors Oposa*. In this case the Court recognized the right of minors to act in court, through their representatives, also on behalf of future generations and their interest in the preservation of tropical forests. The ICJ since has recognized the interests of future generations in the preservation of the environment. First, in its advisory opinion in *Nuclear Weapons* (para. 29) and later in *Gabčíkovo-Nagymaros* (para. 112) it implicitly referred to the principle of inter-generational equity by stating "that the environment is not an abstraction but represents the living space, the quality of life and the very health of human beings, including generations unborn". In *Gabčíkovo-Nagymaros* the ICJ took this to imply, together with the evolution of international environmental law, that environmental impacts should be assessed on a continuous basis (section 4.7.4). It held that "[t]he awareness of the vulnerability of the environment and the recognition that environmental risks have to be assessed on a continuous basis have become much stronger in the years since the Treaty's conclusion [in 1977]". (para. 112).

4.5.6 Intra-generational equity

Intra-generational equity refers to equity between members of the same generation and is particularly relevant in the North–South context. It is linked to the right to development expressed in Principle 3, which as mentioned above is contested, but also to the duty to eradicate poverty contained in Principle 6 of the Rio Declaration. The principle of intra-generational equity serves to point to the inequities in current international economic relations, in particular. As equity towards future generations, equity among the members of the present generation is mentioned as a goal in many MEAs.

While the principle of intra-generational equity clearly points to the enormity of the socio-economic issues at stake in attaining sustainable development, it, like the right to development, has so far not resulted in a general entitlement under international law for poor individuals and groups in society to have their situations alleviated.

The Nagoya Protocol to the Biodiversity Convention provides a concrete example of how the principle of intra-generational equity may be implemented. Of particular relevance is the principle of benefit sharing. Benefit sharing applies to accessing genetic resources and their subsequent use and commercialization. According to the Nagoya Protocol, benefit sharing applies at two levels: at the inter-state level and at the level of indigenous or local communities. At the inter-state level benefit sharing requires that states of origin which provide access to genetic resources and states who obtain access to genetic resources fairly and equitably share the benefits derived from access to the resources (Art. 5(1)). At the level of indigenous or local communities benefit sharing requires that when use is made of their traditional knowledge associated with genetic resources benefits are to be shared in a fair and equitable way with such communities (Art. 5(5)). The Protocol also determines that access to genetic resources shall be based on the prior informed consent, both of the state of origin and of indigenous and local communities involved (Art. 6). In the latter case, the condition applies that communities must have established a right to grant access to such resources for them to benefit from the prior informed consent procedure. In case of access to traditional knowledge associated with genetic resources held by indigenous or local communities their prior informed consent must be obtained (Art.7). The Protocol in several of its provisions requires that each party, state of origin and state whose nationals access genetic resources, adopt legislation and administrative and other measures to implement these provisions related to benefit sharing. The Annex to the Protocol provides a non-exhaustive list of how benefits might be shared, including monetary and non-monetary benefits. It is by way of the requirement to legislate and its Annex that the Nagoya Protocol intends to affect the relationship between actors accessing genetic resources, on the one hand, and indigenous or local communities holding traditional knowledge associated with genetic resources or holding access rights to those resources, on the other hand. The Protocol, however, like other international environmental law treaties, refrains from directly addressing the private sector.

Also note that the prior informed consent procedure in the Nagoya Protocol is to be distinguished from prior informed consent procedures discussed in section 3.5.1 on at least two accounts. First the Nagoya Protocol regulates accessing "a good" that a state or an indigenous or local community holds and payment for obtaining access to the "good" in question and the benefits derived therefrom. The prior informed consent procedures referred to in section 3.5.1 regulate international trade and in particular access to markets. Second, the procedure provided by Nagoya Protocol, as opposed to those discussed in section 3.5.1, is not primarily expert driven. The two types of prior informed consent procedures, however, also share a common trait. Streamlining procedures for accessing a desirable good – genetic resources and markets – though internationally agreed procedures.

4.5.7 Common but differentiated responsibilities

The principle of common but differentiated responsibilities entails that states while striving for common objectives, have different responsibilities depending on their needs, historical contribution to environmental degradation, present contribution to the problem and access to technological and financial resources. It can be regarded as a translation of the principle of intra-generational equity to the inter-state level, in that it requires that the different socio-economic position of states are to be taken into account. It can also be regarded as implementing the principle of inter-generational equity at the inter-state level, in that it prescribes that account be taken of history: past contributions to environmental degradation.

Principle 7 of the Rio Declaration formulates the principle of common but differentiated responsibilities as follows:

> States shall cooperate in a spirit of global partnership to conserve, protect and restore the health and integrity of the Earth's ecosystem. In view of the different contributions to global environmental degradation, States have common but differentiated responsibilities. The developed countries

acknowledge the responsibility that they bear in the international pursuit to sustainable development in view of the pressures their societies place on the global environment and of the technologies and financial resources they command.

Most MEAs, like the Biodiversity Convention, indirectly incorporate the principle of common but differentiated responsibilities by referring to its content. The UNFCCC is the exception in that it includes an explicit reference to the principle in its Article 3.

MEAs implement the principle of common but differentiated responsibilities in several ways. First, MEAs, like the Biodiversity Convention, contain a provision that makes implementation by developing states conditional on developed states meeting their commitments, including their commitments to make available financial resources and technologies to developing states. Second, some MEAs exempt developing states from certain obligations. The emission reduction provisions of the Kyoto Protocol, which only apply to developed and economy in transition states, and not to developing states, provide an example. Third, MEAs may entitle developing states to implement obligations in a phased manner. The ten-year grace period for developing states contained in the Montreal Protocol is an example of the phased application of certain obligations to developing states. Fourth, MEAs require the transfer of funds from developed states to developing states. The financial mechanisms linked to most MEAs serve this purpose, in addition to direct transfers of funds between developed and developing states. These financial mechanisms also provide the basis for linkages that exist between MEAs and financial institutions such as the World Bank and the GEF (section 5.5).

As mentioned above (section 2.4), the principle of common but differentiated obligations currently poses challenges in the relationship between developed and developing states, raising the question what the role of emerging economies should be in MEAs in general and the climate regime in particular (section 3.4.3).

4.6   Due diligence

The principles of no harm, equitable and reasonable use, the common interest of humankind, intra-generational equity, inter-generational equity and common but differentiated responsibilities, discussed in the previous section, indicate what the aim of environmental and natural resources-related policies should be by emphasizing certain relations of independence. However, they do not indicate *when* protective action should be taken or, in legal terms, they do not indicate the due diligence, or standard of care, that may be expected of a state. This is where the prevention principle and the precautionary principle are relevant. They determine the standard due diligence that may be expected of a state.

4.6.1 Prevention principle

The prevention principle is reflected in Principle 2 of the Rio Declaration, quoted above (section 4.5.1). It is generally agreed that the prevention principle imposes an obligation of conduct, instead of an obligation of result. This obligation is closely related to the duties of good neighbourliness stemming from, among others sources, Roman law and related to relations between neighbours and to the obligation to refrain from abuse of rights. It entails that a state must show that it has taken all steps that could reasonably be expected of it to prevent the harm in question. This includes showing that it has taken the necessary steps to ensure that those operating within its jurisdiction, for example operators of industrial plants, have acted to prevent the harm in question.

The specific conduct, or due diligence, that may be expected from a state is to a large extent context dependent, in particular on the nature of the activity and the characteristics of the environment in question. The more risky or dangerous an activity and the more vulnerable the environment, the higher the degree of due diligence and thus preventive action expected from a state. Moreover, the state of scientific knowledge about the environment in question and the availability of technology able to protect that environment also play a role in determining what may reasonably be expected of a state: the more that is known about the vulnerability of an ecosystem and how to protect it, together with the increased availability of technology to protect ecosystems, the more concrete will be the preventive measures required of a state. In addition, the implications of the prevention principle also depend on the development of more technical environmental regulations, for example those regarding BAT and BEP (section 3.4.1). If it is widely agreed, evidenced by, for example, decisions of COPs or subsidiary bodies, national laws and policies or industrial practice, that a certain technology or practice is the best way to protect the environment, it may be expected that this technology or practice will be applied, especially to new activities.

The *Pulp Mills* case however, illustrates that applying BAT may not suffice. In this case Uruguay argued that the pulp mills within its territory were applying BAT and that therefore it had fulfilled its duty to ensure the prevention of environmental harm. The ICJ, however, determined that, although Uruguay had exercised due diligence in preventing environmental harm (para. 265), the obligation to cooperate continued to apply. This obligation requires that other riparian states be consulted and that riparian states together consider all uses of the shared watercourse, including the interests of all states in the watercourse, as well as the protection of the shared watercourse (section 4.7.4). If such consultations and considerations do not take place the use in question may not be equitable and reasonable (section 4.5.2), in spite of the application of BAT (paras. 119–22 and 192–265).

4.6.2   Precautionary principle

In addition to the prevention principle, the precautionary principle determines the due diligence that may be expected of a state, and indirectly of the non-state actors subject to its jurisdiction. It imposes enhanced due diligence in situations of scientific uncertainty. The precautionary principle determines that scientific uncertainty about the causal relationship between an activity or product and (serious or irreversible) harm to the environment shall not be a reason for postponing action to protect the environment. Formulations of the precautionary principle vary from strong formulations that entail a reversal of the burden of proof, to weaker formulations that require a precautionary approach to environmental protection and also refer to cost-effectiveness. Principle 15 of the Rio Declaration provides an example of a weaker formulation. It reads as follows:

> In order to protect the environment, the precautionary approach shall be widely applied by States according to their capabilities. Where there are threats of serious or irreversible damage, lack of full scientific certainty shall not be used as a reason for postponing cost-effective measures to prevent environmental degradation.

Article 2(2)(a) of the OSPAR Convention is an example of a stronger formulation. It reads as follows:

The Contracting Parties shall apply:
(a) the precautionary principle, by virtue of which preventive measures are to be taken when there are reasonable grounds for concern that substances or energy introduced, directly or indirectly, into the marine environment may bring about hazards to human health, harm living resources and marine ecosystems, damage amenities or interfere with other legitimate uses of the sea, even when there is no conclusive evidence of a causal relationship between the inputs and the effects . . .

The precautionary approach is explicitly mentioned in many MEAs. The Stockholm Convention and the Cartagena Protocol, for example, refer to Principle 15 of the Rio Declaration and the precautionary approach in their preambles and in their first articles. The Stockholm Convention and the Fish Stocks Agreement also incorporate precaution in their decision-making procedures. The Stockholm Convention requires the COP when taking decisions to list chemicals on the annexes to the Convention to take into account scientific uncertainty and decide in a precautionary manner (Art. 8(9)) and calls upon its parties to base decisions determining BAT on the costs and benefits involved as well as precaution and prevention (Annex C, Part V(B)). The Fish Stocks Agreement refers to the precautionary approach as a general principle (Art. 5(c)) (section 4.3), and makes it the basis for managing straddling and highly migratory stocks (Art. 6), among others, by introducing precautionary reference points (Annex II) (section 4.3). Article 3(3), on principles, of the UNFCCC is explicit in determining that its parties take precautionary measures. It reads as follows:

The Parties should take precautionary measures to anticipate, prevent or minimize the causes of climate change and mitigate its adverse effects. Where there are threats of serious or irreversible damage, lack of full scientific certainty should not be used as a reason for postponing such measures, taking into account that policies and measures to deal with climate change should be cost-effective so as to ensure global benefits at the lowest possible cost.

The ICJ in *Gabčikovo-Nagymaros* applied the precautionary principle by referring to its content, even if it did not explicitly refer to the principle. In the face of contradictory scientific information the Court held that it "is mindful that, in the field of environmental protection, vigilance and prevention are required on account of the often irreversible character of damage to the environment and of the limitations inherent in the very mechanism of reparation of this type of damage" (para. 140).

The Appellate Body of the WTO *EC–Hormones* did not recognize the principle as a general principle of international law (para. 123) (section 7.4.3). The International Tribunal for the Law of the Sea (ITLOS) applied the principle in the *Southern Bluefin Tuna* cases (Provisional Measures), using the following terms:

> Considering that, in the view of the Tribunal, the parties should in the circumstances [in particular scientific uncertainty and the level of catches, paras. 73–6, EH] act with prudence and caution to ensure that effective conservation measures are taken to prevent serious harm to the stock of southern bluefin tuna. (para. 77)

ITLOS took a similar approach in its 2003 order on Provisional Measures in the case *Concerning Land Reclamation by Singapore in and around the Straits of Johor*. In this case it considered:

> given the possible implications of land reclamation on the marine environment, prudence and caution require that Malaysia and Singapore establish mechanisms for exchanging information and assessing the risks or effects of land reclamation works and devising ways to deal with them in the areas concerned. (para. 99)

The ICJ in *Pulp Mills* furthermore held that "a precautionary approach may be relevant in the interpretation and application of the provisions of the [River Uruguay] Statute" even if "it does not follow that it operates as a reversal of the burden of proof" (para. 164). The first part of the ICJ finding, and the fact that the precautionary approach has been included in numerous treaties and other instruments, prompted the ITLOS Seabed Disputes Chamber, part of the dispute settlement mechanisms available under the LOS Convention, in its 2011 Advisory Opinion on *Responsibilities and Obligations of States Sponsoring Persons and Entities with Respect to Activities in the Area* to remark: "this has initiated a trend towards making this approach part of customary international law" (para. 135). In the same Opinion the Chamber held that Regulations of the International Seabed Authority, incorporating the precautionary approach and referring to Principle 15 of the Rio Declaration, require sponsoring states to apply the precautionary approach. It, moreover, held "that the precautionary approach is also an integral part of the general obligation of due diligence of sponsoring States, which is applicable even outside the scope of the Regulations" (para. 131). The latter suggests that the precautionary approach has attained the status of customary international law, at least in the context of activities in the Area.

The ITLOS finding in its effects is very similar to the finding of the ICJ in *Gabčikovo-Nagymaros* and *Pulp Mills*. In each of these cases environmental concerns are among the elements that trigger the requirement to exchange views and assess environmental consequences. While the precautionary principle does not specify the types of measures that are to be taken, state practice and the above-quoted findings of international courts and tribunals show that prior environmental impact assessments (section 4.7.4) are particularly relevant. Such procedures facilitate considering all relevant factors and, provided they are participatory, enable a wide range of individuals and groups to voice their concerns.

4.7 Operational principles

Besides principles expressing the aims of international environmental law and those addressing due diligence standards that may be expected of a state, international environmental law also harbours a number of principles that indicated *what* is expected of states in general or in specific situations. These more operational principles relate to the need to integrate environmental concerns in all relevant policy areas, the polluter having to pay for harm caused; exchange of information; assessment of environmental impacts; and to transparency, participation and access to justice.

4.7.1 Integration

Principle 4 of the Rio Declaration, quoted in section 4.5.4 above, besides referring to sustainable development, also reflects what is known as the integration principle. In general the integration principle requires that environmental considerations be incorporated into other policy areas. In Principle 4 the specific reference is to the need to incorporate environmental considerations into development policies. The integration principle, however, has found wider reflection in international law, including in the Rio Declaration. The Rio Declaration makes the link to human rights (Principle 1), international trade law (Principle 12) and the law of armed conflict (Principles 24, 25). In the Rio Declaration these links, however, are rather unspecified or weak. This is due to the way in which the other policy areas are referred to: the link remains implicit (Principle 1, for human rights); it remains indeterminate due to the controversies that are prominent in relationships between environmental considerations and the policy area at stake (Principle 12, for trade); or remains exceedingly general (Principles 24 and 25, for the law of armed conflict). The ILA Declaration, much more clearly than the Rio Declaration, points to the other areas of international law and policy that are at stake if sustainable development is to be attained. It refers to international economic and social cooperation (para. 2.3), human rights law (especially para. 5), international investment law (para. 6.3) and international trade law (para. 6.3). The links between international environmental law and a number of other areas of international law will be considered in Chapter 7.

Some MEAs, such as the UNFCCC in its Article 3(4) and the Biodiversity Convention in its Article 6(b), incorporate the integration principle by referring to the need to incorporate the measures or policies adopted within their ambit into other policy areas. The UNFCCC requires states to integrate policies and measures to protect the climate system in national development programmes. The Biodiversity Convention requires states to "integrate the conservation and sustainable use of biological diversity into relevant sectoral or cross-sectoral plans, programmes and policies". A holistic version of the integration principle, in the sense that it refers to environmental protection in general, which also makes explicit the aim of integration is found in Article 11 of the 2007 Treaty on the Functioning of the European Union. It reads as follows:

> Environmental protection requirements must be integrated into the definition and implementation of the Union's policies and activities, in particular with a view to promoting sustainable development.

4.7.2 Polluter pays

The polluter pays principle is one of the older principles that has been promoted by way of international environmental law. It was developed under the auspices of the OECD during the 1970s.[1] The principle determines that the perpetrator of pollution should pay for the environmental damage that its activity generates. In other words, it should

---

1 OECD, *The Polluter Pays Principle: Definition, Analysis, Implementation* (OECD, 1975).

not be public funds that pay for the rehabilitation of polluted ecosystems; such costs should instead be defrayed to and internalized by the polluter.

The principle was not meant to apply at the inter-state level, but meant for states to implement vis-à-vis private actors either at the national level or at the international level; the latter by agreements such as the civil liability conventions applicable to maritime transport and the production of nuclear energy (sections 3.3.1, 3.3.2). Because a strict interpretation of the principle would result in subsidies to relatively environmental-friendly activities being prohibited, the principle is often formulated in terms of the internalization of environmental costs. This is also the formulation found in the Rio Declaration. Its Principle 16 states that:

> National authorities should endeavour to promote the internalization of environmental costs and the use of economic instruments, taking into account the approach that the polluter should, in principle, bear the cost of pollution, with due regard to the public interest and without distorting international trade and investment.

While the principle seems straightforward and easy to apply it also raises a number of questions. For example, who is the polluter in case of an accident with an oil tanker? The ship owner, ship operator or the cargo owner? Similarly, who is the polluter in case of the emission of GHGs in the production of electricity? The power plant in question or the consumers of the electricity? And, who is the consumer of the electricity? The industrial plant that consumes electricity to produce cars or the consumers of the cars? The polluter pays principle ultimately suggest that it is the consumer that is to pay for harm to the environment; however, in order for that to happen the costs of polluting the environment need to be borne by successive producers of a product or carriers of a polluting substance. In case of accidental vessel source pollution the international civil liability conventions distribute liabilities between ship owners (Civil Liability Convention) and cargo owners (Fund Convention), the costs of which presumably will be reflected in the price of oil. Discussions regarding the introduction of a carbon tax illustrate how difficult it may be actually to have the polluter, instead of public funds, pay for, for example, climate change adaptation measures.

4.7.3 Exchange of information

Most MEAs contain general provisions requiring the exchange of information among their parties and usually also contain provisions which highlight the special requirements of developing countries in this respect. The latter type of provision requires the transfer of information, scientific understanding and technology, or at least knowledge about technology, to developing states. Principle 9 of the Rio Declaration reflects in particular the latter concerns. It provides that:

> States should cooperate to strengthen endogenous capacity-building for sustainable development by improving scientific understanding through exchanges of scientific and technological knowledge, and by enhancing the development, adaptation, diffusion and transfer of technologies, including new and innovative technologies.

The Biodiversity Convention in its Article 17 provides a general commitment to exchange information and in its Article 18 sets out the commitment to engage in scientific and technical cooperation, among others through a clearing-house mechanism established within the biodiversity regime. Clearing-house mechanisms as a means of exchanging information are part of many MEAs and provide, among other things, a platform for exchanging best practices.

Article 4(2)(h) of the Basel Convention provides an example of a provision on the exchange of information which is directly linked to the aim of the Convention: sound management of hazardous and other wastes. It reads as follows:

> Co-operate in activities with other Parties and interested organizations, directly and through the Secretariat, including the dissemination of information on the transboundary movement of hazardous wastes and other wastes, in order to improve the environmentally sound management of such wastes and to achieve the prevention of illegal traffic.

The Basel Convention, in its Article 13, further develops this obligation by specifying the type of information the parties are to exchange. This exchange of information is in addition to the information that parties exchange in the prior informed consent procedure, which applies to trade in hazardous wastes. Prior informed consent procedures for their effectiveness of course crucially depend on the exchange of information (section 3.5.1).

Besides the above provisions, many MEAs contain two further types of provision on the exchange of information. The first type of provision applies to accidents or emergencies that are likely to have significant adverse transboundary effects (section 3.3); the second to activities in general that may have adverse transboundary effects. The latter are particularly relevant in the context of environmental impact assessments (section 4.7.4).

4.7.3.1   Notification in case of emergencies

Principle 18 of the Rio Declaration concerns the requirement to notify in case of emergencies or accidents. It reads as follows:

> States shall immediately notify other States of any natural disasters or other emergencies that are likely to produce sudden harmful effects on the environment of those States. Every effort shall be made by the international community to help States so afflicted.

Examples of MEAs which contain similar provisions are the LOS Convention (Art. 198), the Basel Convention (Art. 13(1)), the Biodiversity Convention (Art. 14(1(d))) and the Watercourses Convention (Art. 28). One of the aspects to note with regard to these provisions is that the degree of harm that triggers the duty to notify differs significantly (varying from "harmful" to "imminent" or "grave") as does the object that may be harmed (varying from "the environment" to "another state"). Principle 18 refers to "harmful effects on the environment of" other states; the LOS Convention refers to the marine environment which "is in imminent danger of being damaged or has been damaged by pollution" (Art. 198); the Basel Convention refers to "risks to human health and the environment in other States" (Art. 13(1)); the Biodiversity Convention refers to "imminent or grave danger or damage, originating under its jurisdiction or control, to biological diversity within the area under jurisdiction of other States or in areas beyond the limits of national jurisdiction" (Art. 14(1)(d)); while the Watercourses Convention refers to emergencies that pose "an imminent threat of causing, serious harm to watercourse States or other States" (Art. 28(1)).

Specific agreements dealing with emergency situations have also been adopted. These include the Notification Convention, applicable to emergencies with nuclear plants (section 3.3.1), the Industrial Accidents Convention (section 3.3.3), as well as conventions that cover accidental marine pollution from vessels (section 3.3.2). These agreements provide comprehensive notification and consultation regimes as well as provisions on cooperation in case of an emergency.

4.7.3.2   *Notification and consultation in case of activities*

Principle 19 of the Rio Declaration formulates the obligation of states to notify and consult each other in case they plan to engage in an activity that may cause significant adverse transboundary effects:

> States shall provide prior and timely notification and relevant information to potentially affected States on activities that may have a significant adverse transboundary environmental effect and shall consult with those States at an early stage and in good faith.

Many watercourse conventions contain similar obligations. Relevant examples are the Watercourses Convention (Arts.11–19); the UNECE 1992 Helsinki Water Convention (Art. 9(2)(h)); the 2000 Southern African Development Community (SADC) Water Protocol (Art. 4(1)); and 2003 Protocol for Sustainable Development of Lake Victoria Basin (Art. 13). Other examples of conventions that contain such provisions are the Biodiversity Convention (Art. 14(1)(c)) and the Revised African Nature Conservation Convention (Art. XXII(2)(b)). While these examples concern resource-specific instruments, the 2001 International Law Commission's (ILC) Articles on the Prevention of Transboundary Harm, like the Rio Declaration, addresses notification and consultation for transboundary effects in general (Arts. 8, 9, 10). Most instruments require that transboundary impacts be assessed, without necessarily specifying that an environmental impact assessment (EIA), a specific procedure for assessing environmental impacts, be conducted (section 4.7.4). Most instruments also require consultation among the states concerned and many provide at least some conditions regarding the manner in which the consultation process is to be conducted. In addition some instruments, such as the UNECE Helsinki Water Convention (Art. 11) and the ILC Articles on the Prevention of Transboundary Harm (Art. 12), require states to monitor activities once implemented.

4.7.4   Assessment of environmental impacts

EIA and strategic environmental assessment (SEA) procedures involve specific decision-making processes for assessing the consequences of activities, plans or programmes for human health and the environment. EIA involves decisions to engage in concrete activities, such as the building of a major infrastructure project or a nuclear power plant. SEA involves decisions on plans and programmes that set parameters for future activities, for example on the role of nuclear energy in a state's energy supply or on a process for selecting and protecting nature conservation areas. EIA and SEA serve to facilitate public participation in decision-making, to provide decision-makers with relevant information, require that decision-makers take into account the information received, and account for how they have taken that information into account. Ultimately, the aim of these procedures is to generate better informed and more sustainable decisions on projects that may affect the environment.

The Rio Declaration in its Principle 17 refers to EIA only. It reads as follows:

> Environmental impact assessment, as a national instrument, shall be undertaken for proposed activities that are likely to have a significant adverse impact on the environment and are subject to a decision of a competent national authority.

The duty to assess the environmental consequences of projects that may harm the environment, including the assessment of transboundary impacts, is now widely accepted, as the above-quoted decision in *Gabčikovo-Nagymaros* shows (section 4.5.5). Moreover, in *Pulp Mills*, the ICJ found that requirements regarding the conduct of an environmental assessment may be violated if procedural standards, for example regarding the proper notification and consultation of the other party, have not been met (paras. 112–22) (section 4.5.2). The ICJ thus determined that procedural requirements are relevant in their own right, irrespective of compliance with substantive standards, such as the application of BAT (section 3.4.1).

As illustrated in the previous section, many environmental instruments contain provisions requiring that transboundary environmental impacts be assessed as part of a notification and consultation process. However, it is not always clear whether reference is to the assessment of environmental impacts, including transboundary impacts, or whether it is to an EIA-procedure as described above. Article 206 of the 1982 LOS Convention, for example, requires that the potential effects of activities on the marine environment be assessed. Article 8 of the Antarctic Environmental Protocol determines that the EIA procedure sets out in its Annex I be applied to specific activities. The LOS Convention, then, contains a general obligation to assess environmental impacts, while the Antarctic Environmental Protocol clearly refers to an EIA procedure. References to EIA procedures are also contained in UNEPs 1987 Goals and Principles of EIA, and the 2002 and 2008 resolutions on EIA and SEA guidelines adopted by the COP of the Ramsar Convention. These resolutions are noteworthy because they do not themselves develop EIA and SEA procedures. Instead they approve for implementation by parties to the Ramsar Convention, the guidelines developed for EIA and SEA as adopted within the framework of the Biodiversity Convention. This development illustrates a linkage between the two regimes (section 5.4). Multilateral development banks, such as the World Bank, have also incorporated EIA procedures in their OP&Ps, which are to be applied to projects in which they invest. In addition, certification schemes, such as the one operated by the FSC, use impact assessment procedures to assess the environmental and social consequences of projects that apply for the certification.

The UNECE 1991 Espoo Convention on EIA and its 2003 SEA Protocol constitute a regional regime that prescribes the conduct of EIA and SEA procedures in transboundary contexts. The Espoo regime determines how EIA and SEA procedures are to be conducted and includes standards for the conduct of transboundary consultation, including public consultation (Art. 4(1) Espoo Convention; Art. 10(4) SEA Protocol). The Espoo Convention also determines that the states involved in a transboundary EIA, at the request of one of them, are to set up a post-project analysis plan for monitoring the execution of activities that have been subjected to EIA (Art. 7), and the SEA Protocol provides that each party will monitor the environmental impacts of plans or programmes that are implemented after having been subjected to SEA (Art. 12). These instruments thereby incorporate the importance of continuous environmental assessment, referred to by the ICJ in *Gabčikovo-Nagymaros* (section 4.5.5)

In addition to EIA and SEA procedures, risk assessment procedures are part of regimes that address trade in hazardous substances. Risk assessments tend to be expert-based and science-driven procedures. Contrary to EIA and SEA procedures, risk assessment procedures do not generally involve public participation. Risk assessments are part of the prior informed consent procedures to implement, for example, the Stockholm and Rotterdam Conventions as well as the Cartagena Protocol (section 3.5.1). Risk assessments are also part of the 1995

WTO Agreement on Sanitary and Phytosanitary Measures (SPS Agreement). Under the SPS Agreement risk assessments, provided that certain conditions are met, may serve to justify the introduction of trade restrictive measures by a member state in order to protect human, animal or plant life or health (section 7.4.3).

4.7.5 Transparency, participation and access to justice

Principle 10 of the Rio Declaration provides as follows:

> Environmental issues are best handled with participation of all concerned citizens, at the relevant level. At the national level, each individual shall have appropriate access to information concerning the environment that is held by public authorities, including information on hazardous materials and activities in their communities, and the opportunity to participate in decision-making processes. States shall facilitate and encourage public awareness and participation by making information widely available. Effective access to judicial and administrative proceedings, including redress and remedy, shall be provided.

Principle 10, if translated into entitlements language, does not recognize a right to a clean or healthy environment, instead it recognizes procedural rights to information, participation in decision-making and review in environmental matters. The thinking behind Principle 10 might be captured as follows: individuals ultimately undergo the negative consequences of unsustainable activities and environmental degradation, therefore if individuals have access to these three procedural rights they will be able to voice their interests, and as a consequence uphold their substantive rights and the environment will be better protected. Note that Principle 10 in its first sentence provides a broad entitlement to participation at the relevant level and then details that entitlement for the national level of decision-making.

Since the Rio Conference transparency of and participation in international environmental decision-making has certainly increased, perhaps most clearly reflected by the information that is readily available on the website of relevant MEAs and international organizations and in the large numbers and the diversity of observers that participate in international environmental negotiations. In addition, stakeholder participation is widely recognized as crucial for the protection of species, habitats and ecosystems in decisions taken within relevant MEAs, such as the Biodiversity Convention and the Bonn Convention. Moreover, some MEAs and international organizations regularly submit draft decisions or plans to public comment through their websites. A relevant example is the CDM's Executive Board policy on stakeholder interaction in the context of which roundtables are regularly held and calls for public input into regulatory documents are regularly issued.

Principle 10 has not been further developed into a global MEA. However, it is worthy of note that in *Pulp Mills* Argentina and Uruguay did not disagree that the affected population on both sides of the border should have been consulted in the conduct of the EIA procedure, even if they disagreed as to how this should have been done (paras. 215–19).

Principle 10 has found implementation at the international level in four distinct ways. First, Principle 10 is at the basis of the Aarhus Convention, which developed the principle in its three pillars – transparency, participation in decision-making and access to justice – and established a compliance committee where individuals and groups in society can complain if their rights under these three pillars have not been complied with (section 6.4.2). Second, IDBs, such as the World Bank, have incorporated standards regarding access to information and participation in decision-making in their OP&Ps that apply to projects they invest in. For example, the World Bank's policy on environmental assessment prescribes public participation for potentially affected groups and local NGOs and requires that these groups be given access to information. In addition, development banks have implemented the access to justice entitlement by establishing compliance mechanisms before which individuals and groups in society can complain if they suffer or may suffer harm as a result of the policies of the Bank in question not being properly implemented. An example of such a mechanism is the World Bank Inspection Panel (section 6.4.1). Third, stakeholder organizations, such as the FSC, implement standards regarding transparency, participation and access to justice (section 6.4.3). Fourth, human rights bodies have widely recognized procedural environmental rights as part of substantive human rights, the right to private and family life in particular (section 7.2.3).

4.8   Assessment

This chapter illustrates how the complex social-ecological problems that emerged from the preceding chapters find resonance in international environmental law principles. It shows that the socio-economic aspects of these problems are reflected in relevant principles, even if these principles do not capture the role of the private sector. Moreover, how the human/environment interface might be mediated remains unaddressed by environmental law principles. Lastly, this chapter illustrates a remarkable development in the law of international watercourses, and perhaps beyond this area of law, by the ICJ's interpretation of environmental law principles. These points are considered below.

The principles of sustainable development and the common concern of humankind recognize that environmental problems involve complex socio-economic connections between humans, including spatially and in terms of time. The principle of intra-generational equity addresses the spatial aspect; the principle of inter-generational equity the time aspect. The principle of common but differentiated responsibilities, furthermore, factors socio-economic inequalities at the inter-state level into legal relationships by requiring that states take these inequalities into account in the design and implementation of the legal regimes that address complex environmental problems. These principles in addressing relations of independence, in particular in the North–South context, harbour a promise of justice (section 2.4).

The private sector is a noteworthy absentee at the level of principles that address relations of interdependence in environmental law. Only the Nagoya Protocol conceptualizes the role of the private sector by way of the concept of benefit sharing, based on the principle of intra-generational equity, even if it does so indirectly by requiring states to legislate so as to realize benefit sharing between private sector actors and indigenous and local communities (section 4.5.6). The under-conceptualization of the private sector is remarkable given the conceptualization of environmental problems as socio-economic problems. Can socio-economic problems be addressed without a meaningful understanding of how private sector actors, given their social and economic influence, fit the picture conceptually? Might the effect of this lack of conceptualization be that private sector actors when they act transnationally or in international or global contexts largely act in a legal vacuum, unless national law is able to capture their activities or they subscribe to certification regimes such as the one operated by the FSC?

How the human/environment interface might be mediated in terms of law remains unaddressed by environmental law principles. In other words, how humans and their socio-economic systems relate to the environment is not conceptualized by these principles, beyond their anthropocentric implications. Addressing this interface would require incorporating ethical reflection in international environmental law, for example on how we relate to the Earth's systems (section 1.2.1). That is a tall order in a significantly divided world in which consensus about, for example, what constitute environmentally detrimental subsidies has not been attained (section 3.6.2).

At the level of transboundary resources, or at least for international watercourses, a remarkable development has taken place by way of the interpretation of international environmental law principles. Based on the case law of the ICJ, for the law on international watercourses, it is clear that equitable and reasonable use with the aim of attaining optimal and sustainable utilization of the resource is to be the overarching goal, requiring meaningful consultation among the states involved. Moreover, such consultations involve the complex task of balancing economic development and environmental protection and thereby the aim of attaining sustainable development. It is also clear that the environmental consequences of activities are to be assessed through processes of notification and consultation that take place prior to the project being authorized and with the involvement of individuals and groups in society, also those located across a state border. Moreover, lack of consultation and participation cannot be justified by the argument that the no harm principle has been complied with, for example because BAT is being employed. These considerations suggest what constitutes good governance in relation to the uses of an international watercourse and perhaps transboundary resources and environments more in general. Lastly, based on case law, the precautionary principle is to be part of what constitute good governance arrangements for transboundary resources and environments as well as for the Area, and perhaps of other regimes related to the global commons.

5 Institutional structures

5.1 Introduction

Several institutional patterns are discernible, if one takes a helicopter view of the decision-making processes and actors involved in the development of international environmental policy and law. MEAs are the most salient element in these patterns. An MEA provides a framework for further cooperation among states parties, often together with other actors, hence the denomination framework conventions. MEAs structure further cooperation in two distinct ways. Some MEAs require that their content be developed in decision-making among groups of its states parties in the context of environments or species that they share. In this case normative development takes place within these more localized agreements. An example of this type of MEAs is the Watercourses Convention, which requires implementation at the level of international watercourses. Other MEAs establish a basic institutional structure and require further decision-making at the global or regional level. In this case normative development of the regime evolves by way of these global or regional decision-making processes. Examples of this type of MEA are, at the global level, CITES, the UNFCCC, the Stockholm Convention and, at the regional level, the LRTAP and Aarhus Conventions. The Ramsar Convention and the Bonn Convention are examples of conventions that combine the two approaches. The former provides a global framework for further development of, among other things, standards regarding the wise use of wetlands and its Article 5 requires states to cooperate with respect to the conservation of shared wetlands. The latter provides a global framework for decision-making on migratory species and requires states that share the migratory range of a species to cooperate.

A salient difference between the institutional structures of these two types of MEAs is that MEAs that require decision-making at the global or regional level develop a complex and dynamic institutional structure for decision-making at those levels, whereas MEAs that require international decision-making at the locality of a shared environment or species tend to have a rather lean institutional structure at the global level. The Watercourses Convention, for example, does not foresee the establishment of any institutions at the global level of decision-making. Presumably, its parties, as the parties to the LOS Convention and the Fish Stocks Agreement have been doing, will meet based on resolutions adopted by UNGA. These meetings, contrary to the COPs or MEAs that require decision-making at the global or regional level, do not generally engage in decision-making that results in further normative development of the regime, that is unless they adopt a new treaty instrument, such as the Fish Stocks Agreement. Normative development, for MEAs that require localized international decision-making, takes place in the forums established pursuant to the agreements concluded at the level of the shared environment or species, resulting in complex and dynamic institutional structures for decision-making at that level. MEAs that combine both approaches generate institutional complexity and dynamics at both levels.

Other institutional patterns that are discernible are the links between MEAs and international organizations, often through their secretariats, and the links between MEAs and international financial institutions, the World Bank in particular. In addition, MEAs in various ways interact with non-state actors, both NGOs and the private sector.

These different institutional patterns give rise to a variety of settings in which the development of international environmental law takes place. The resulting institutional complexity in practice has resulted in disagreements regarding the competence of a regime to regulate a certain activity (section 3.5.3) and has been criticized for lack of coordination. This chapter examines the patterns identified above. In its assessment it discusses some of the underlying reasons why the competences of MEAs have been the subject of debate and considers whether the institutional system for developing international environmental law is as disjointed as has been suggested.

This chapter first considers MEAs that prescribe localized international decision-making. It then considers MEAs that prescribe decision-making at the global or regional level. Thereafter the chapter considers institutional linkages among MEAs and between MEAs and international organizations. Finally, the chapter focuses on the interlinkages that exist between MEAs, financial mechanisms and IDBs.

5.2 MEAs and localized international decision-making

Examples of MEAs that require localized international decision-making are the aforementioned Watercourses Convention; the Bonn Convention; the LOS Convention as related to shared fish stocks in combination with the Fish Stocks Agreement; and the provisions of the LOS Convention on the prevention of marine pollution. Both in case of fisheries and prevention of marine pollution, the LOS Convention also determines that particular concerns are to be addressed by way of decision-making within global institutions such as the International Whaling Commission (IWC) and the IMO.

MEAs that require localized decision-making usually provide general principles and sometimes minimum standards that states are to implement in agreements applicable to the environment or species in question. The LOS Convention, for example, for the prevention of marine pollution provides the following as a general principle.

> States shall take, individually or jointly as appropriate, all measures consistent with this Convention that are necessary to prevent, reduce and control pollution of the marine environment from any source, using for this purpose the best practicable means at their disposal and in accordance with their capabilities, and they shall endeavour to harmonize their policies in this connection. (Art. 194(1))

More concrete standards are the types of measures that states are to take with respect to endangered migratory species set out in the Bonn Convention (section 5.2.2.) and the precautionary conservation and management system set out in the Fish Stocks Agreement (section 5.2.3). The Watercourses Convention is a bit odd in this respect. On the one hand, it has rather strong provisions on equitable and reasonable use and also on the protection of the environment (sections 4.5.2, 5.2.1). On the other hand, its Article 3(3) provides that watercourse states, provided they agree, may in a watercourse agreement "adjust" the standards set out in the Convention. These standards thus do not have the legal status of minimum standards. Two regional conventions, the Helsinki Water Convention and the SADC Water Protocol take a different approach. They set minimum standards both for how individual states manage an international watercourse (Part I, Helsinki Water Convention; Art. 3, SADC Water Protocol) and for the cooperation that states sharing a watercourse are to engage in (Part II, Helsinki Water Convention; Art. 4, SADC Water Protocol).

MEAs that require localized decision-making, structure institutional development at the localized level by identifying the states that have an interest in the shared environment or species and by determining that it is these states that should cooperate. Some MEAs also determine the tasks and functions of cooperation at the localized level. The localized institutions that are established pursuant to these MEAs, qua institutional complexity, often resemble MEAs that require decision-making at the global or regional levels in that they operate through a plenary body, a number of subsidiary bodies and engage with a large number of other actors, including international organizations, NGOs and private sector actors. In order to provide insight into how MEAs that require localized decision-making structure cooperation the regimes for international watercourses, migratory species, shared marine fisheries resources and the prevention of marine pollution will be considered below.

5.2.1   International watercourses

The Watercourses Convention identifies all states that share a watercourse as states that have an interest in the watercourse and that should cooperate, even if a limited number of watercourse states may conclude agreements among themselves (Art. 4). The Watercourses Convention suggests that it may be useful to establish joint mechanisms or commissions to institutionalize cooperation, but it does not require states to do so (Art. 8(2)). Examples of agreements in which states engage in cooperation at the level of the watercourse and which have institutionalized cooperation are many and often predate the Watercourses Convention. They include the Great Lakes Agreement; the River Uruguay Statute; the 1995 Agreement on the Mekong River, with cooperation in the lower Mekong River dating back to the 1950s; the 1999 Rhine Convention, whose origins can be traced to agreements concluded since 1963; and the 2003 Agreement on the Limpopo Commission, with institutionalized cooperation dating back to 1986.

5.2.2   Migratory species

The Bonn Convention identifies the states that are located within the migratory range of a species as interested parties and as those who should cooperate; it refers to them as "Range States" (Arts. 1(h), 4). The Convention provides two ways in which range states may institutionalize their cooperation, by concluding so-called "AGREEMENTS" (Art.

4(3)) or engaging in "joint action" (Art. 4(4)). Both requirements are formulated as obligations of effort. AGREEMENTS are legally binding arrangements for which the Bonn Convention provides guidelines (Art. 5); joint action are non-legally binding arrangements and in practice have been concluded by way of MOUs. MOUs, as opposed to AGREEMENTS, have also been signed by the Bonn Convention secretariat and by NGOs. Some arrangements concluded under the auspices of the Bonn Convention bring together smaller groups of neighbouring states through whose territory a species migrates; others cover vast areas bringing together states from various continents. Examples of the former include the 1990 Wadden Sea Seals Agreement, concluded between Denmark, Germany and the Netherlands; the 2008 MOU on High Andean Flamingos, concluded between Bolivia, Chile and Peru, but not by Argentina which is also a range state; and the 2005 MOU on West African Populations of the African Elephant, signed by all 13 range states. Examples of arrangements that cover vast areas, even if not all range states are a party to them, are the 1996 African–Eurasian Waterbirds Agreement, which brings together states from Africa, Europe, the Middle East, Central Asia and Canada and Greenland and the 1994 MOU on the Slender-billed Curlew, which brings together states from Africa, Asia and Europe.

5.2.3   Shared marine fisheries resources

The LOS Convention provides the jurisdictional framework for managing marine fisheries resources. It does so based on identifying the states that are entitled to exercise jurisdiction over fishing activities in certain ocean areas. Based on these provisions coastal states are to regulate fishing activities, also those by vessels flying a foreign flag, in archipelagic waters (Arts. 49, 51), the territorial sea (Art. 2) and the exclusive economic zone (EEZ) (Art. 56(1)(a)); and flag states are to regulate fishing activities of vessels flying their flag on the high seas (Art. 116). As mentioned above, the freedom of fishing applicable on the high seas and also MSY-based fisheries management, prescribed for both the EEZ and the high seas (Art. 61(3) and 119) have been criticized for not contributing to sustainable fishing activities (section 3.6.1).

In addition to the jurisdictional zones mentioned above, the LOS Convention identifies seven types of shared fisheries resources and for each type of fisheries resource the interested states which are to cooperate in their management. The seven types of shared fisheries resources are:

- stocks that migrate between EEZs (Art. 63(1));
- straddling stocks or stocks that migrate between an EEZ and the high seas (Art. 63(2));
- highly migratory species, in particular tuna, which migrate over large distances (Art. 64, Annex I);
- marine mammals (Art. 65);
- anadromous stocks, salmon and salmon-like species, which are born and spawn in rivers and spend their life at sea (Art. 66);
- catadromous stocks, eel and eel-like species, which are born and spawn at sea and spend their life in inland waters (Art. 67); and
- fish stocks located in the high seas (Art. 118).

The obligation to cooperate in Article 63 is formulated as an obligation of effort ("shall seek to agree"); the other articles formulate obligations or result in the sense that they require states to cooperate ("shall cooperate" or "shall be regulated by agreement").

In case of marine mammals, Article 65 entitles coastal states and international organizations to regulate their exploitation more strictly than is required for fish stocks, thus pointing to the need for their conservation. For cetaceans, Article 65 directs states to "work through the appropriate international organizations for their conservation, management and study". It is generally agreed that this is an implicit reference to the IWC. The provision is also an example of how an MEA may require that a particular activity, in this case whaling, be addressed by global decision-making but by an institution that it does not itself establish. Other regional agreements that aim to preserve marine mammals are the 1992 Agreement on Marine Mammals in the North Atlantic, the 1991 Agreement on Small Cetaceans of the Baltic and North Seas, which in 2008 was amended to cover also the North–East Atlantic and Irish Seas, and the 1996 Agreement on Cetaceans of the Black Sea, Mediterranean Sea and Contiguous Atlantic Area. The latter two are agreements concluded pursuant to the Bonn Convention (section 5.2.2).

The other provisions of the LOS Convention on shared fish stocks use two criteria to identify the states that have an interest in the stock and that are to cooperate: states in whose waters the stock spends part of its life cycle and states whose vessels fish the stock. For straddling and highly migratory species the Fish Stocks Agreement further defines how states are to cooperate both substantively and institutionally. Substantively, it requires coastal and fishing states to, among other things, implement a precautionary conservation and management regime. Institutionally, it requires these states to enter into arrangements or establish a regional fisheries management organization (RFMO) (Art. 8(1)). The Fish Stocks Agreement also determines the types of issues that should be considered by and the functions of an arrangement or RFMO (Arts. 9–14).

A large number of RFMOs, many whose origins can be traced to before the adoption of the LOS Convention, implement the provisions of the LOS Convention concerning shared fish stocks and those of the Fish Stocks Agreement. Some of these regional agreements are stock-specific; others apply to all fish stocks in a specific geographical area. The Northwest Atlantic Fisheries Organization, which is among the oldest RFMOs, dating back to 1949, regulates fisheries for straddling stocks in high seas areas adjacent to coastal state's EEZs in the Northwest Atlantic. The South East Atlantic Fisheries Organization similarly regulates high seas fishing, but for both straddling and highly migratory stocks.

There are also RFMOs that regulate fishing for highly migratory stocks only, including the Western and Central Pacific Fisheries Commission, the Commission for the Conservation of Southern Bluefin Tuna, the Inter-American Tropical Tuna Commission, the Indian Ocean Tuna Commission and the International Commission for the Conservation of Atlantic Tunas. The Pacific Island Forum Fisheries Agency also relates to highly migratory stocks, but its aims differ from those of the commissions mentioned above. It is an organization in which small Pacific island states unite forces both for managing highly migratory stocks in their EEZs, including negotiating access arrangements with foreign flag vessels, and for developing their positions in relevant international tuna commissions, in particular the Western and Central Pacific Fisheries Commission.

Fisheries for anadromous species are addressed by, for example, the North Atlantic Salmon Conservation Organization, the North Pacific Anadromous Fish Commission and the Pacific Salmon Commission. Fisheries for catadromous species, to the best of this author's knowledge, have not been addressed by species-specific agreements. However, catadromous species are protected by the activities undertaken pursuant to the 2014 Hamilton Declaration on the Sargasso Sea. The Sargasso Sea is a high seas area in the middle of the North Atlantic Ocean, east of Bermuda, which is known for its floating islands of seaweed, *Sargassum*, in which eel populations from North America and Europe spawn.

While some high seas areas, such as the Northwest Atlantic, the Southern Ocean and the Southeast Atlantic Ocean, are covered by RFMOs or arrangements that address fisheries in general, other high seas areas, such as the Central Pacific Ocean and Southwest Atlantic Ocean, are not. The latter is problematic given the discovery of rich fishing grounds in the deep-sea during the 1980s. Many deep-sea fishing activities take place by way of bottom trawling, a fishing method that is particularly damaging for the ecosystems involved and their biodiversity. In 2008 the FAO adopted the International Guidelines on High Seas Deep-sea Fisheries, which, based on the precautionary approach reflected in the Fish Stocks Agreement and the EAF (para. 12), introduced management measures for deep-sea bottom trawling. In June 2015 the UNGA adopted a resolution that aims to build on the FAO Guidelines by developing a legally binding instrument on high seas deep-sea fisheries under the LOS Convention (UNGA Res. 69/292). The preparatory committee established by the resolution is to report to the UNGA by the end of 2017. These decisions illustrate how normative development may take place at the global level in interaction between an international organization, the FAO, and the UNGA with regard to a regime, the LOS Convention, which in principle "delegates" regulation to regional fisheries bodies.

5.2.4   Preventing marine pollution

The LOS Convention, in Part XII, for purposes of the prevention of marine pollution identifies interested states and thus the states that should cooperate based on six sources of marine pollution. The six sources are

- land-based activities;
- seabed activities subject to national jurisdiction, especially oil and gas exploitation;
- activities in the Area, especially deep seabed mining;
- dumping, including incineration, of waste at sea;
- operational and accidental vessel source pollution; and
- atmospheric pollution.

For each source of marine pollution the LOS Convention determines which states have legislative competence (Arts. 207–12) and which have enforcement competence (Arts. 213–22), based on various combinations of port, coastal and flag state jurisdiction. Two types of pollution, vessel source pollution and pollution from activities in the Area, are to be regulated by way of global decision-making by, respectively, the IMO and the International Seabed Authority. For the other sources of marine pollution the LOS Convention imposes an obligation of effort on relevant states to cooperate in the development of global and regional standards, practices and procedures to prevent, reduce and control them. With respect to dumping and incineration at sea the London Convention (section 3.4.2) provides the global instrument. Land-based atmospheric pollution is regulated through the climate change regime, while GHG emissions from shipping have been incorporated into the MARPOL Convention, by way of its Annex VI on air pollution (section 3.3.2). A global instrument for land-based sources of marine pollution has not been adopted.

At the regional level pollution from dumping, land-based sources and vessel source pollution, involving accidental pollution or cooperation in enforcing IMO standards, have been addressed since the 1970s. Relevant agreements for the Northeast Atlantic are the OSPAR Convention, whose origins can be traced to 1972, and the 1969 Bonn Agreement, expanded to include other harmful substances in 1983. For the Baltic Sea the relevant agreement is the Helsinki Convention, whose origins can be traced to 1974. Many other regional sea conventions find their origin in UNEP's Regional Seas Programme, established in 1974. Thirteen regional seas programmes originated in the UNEP programme. They cover the Black Sea, Wider Caribbean, East Asian Seas, Eastern Africa, South Asian Seas, ROPME Sea Area (Arabian/Persian Gulf area), Mediterranean, Northeast Pacific, Northwest Pacific, Red Sea and Gulf of Aden, Southeast Pacific, Pacific, and Western Africa. In addition, marine pollution is addressed in conventions related to the Caspian Sea, the Arctic and the Antarctic.

More recently, regional sea conventions, in addition to land-based sources, dumping and vessel source pollution, have also addressed issues such as coastal zone management, protected areas, trade in hazardous waste, climate change and ecosystem-based management. Since large amounts of land-based marine pollution reach the marine environment via rivers, land-based sources of marine pollution are also controlled by measures to reduce pollution adopted within agreements related to international watercourses (section 5.2.1). In addition to the above, a worldwide system of port state control has been developed based on regional MOUs by way of which states agree to inspect and report on foreign flag ships that enter their ports and do not meet international standards regarding maritime safety or the prevention of vessel source pollution. The first agreement of this nature was the 1982 Paris MOU on Port State Control, which currently covers European coastal states and Canada. At present nine regional MOUs on port state control have been concluded. The institutions established pursuant to these MOUs coordinate their activities, also with the United States, which is not a party to any of the MOUs, and engage with the IMO (section 3.3.2).

As mentioned above, one of the threats currently facing the marine environment consists of the plastics circulating the world's oceans (section 3.2). While their removal is problematic (section 4.5.3), preventing plastics from entering the marine environment is now being addressed by regional sea conventions. The OSPAR Commission, for example, in 2014 adopted the Regional Action Plan for the Prevention and Management of Marine Litter in the North-East Atlantic. Based on this plan states intend to, among other activities, explore possible ways of reducing the use of nanoplastics in cosmetics as well as ways of removing plastics from the marine environment.

5.3 MEAs prescribing globalized international decision-making

Regimes that require decision-making at the global level contain concrete obligations either in the treaty establishing the regime, such as the Basel Convention or the Rotterdam Convention, or in Protocols adopted pursuant to the treaty establishing the regime, such as the Kyoto Protocol to the UNFCCC or the Cartagena Protocol to the Biodiversity Convention. The institutional structure established by MEAs that require global decision-making show a great deal of similarity. It tends to consist of a plenary main decision-making body, a number of standing and ad hoc subsidiary bodies and a secretariat. At the top of the decision-making process is the plenary body, usually called the COP for the basic treaty and meeting of the parties (MOP) or conference of the parties acting as the meeting of the parties (CMP) for protocols. All states parties to an MEA or protocol are members of these plenary bodies, whose meetings are also attended by a large number of observers. Observers normally include states that are not parties to the instrument in question, international organizations, the secretariats of other MEAs, NGOs and private sector representatives.

In these plenary bodies, here collectively referred to as COPs, each state has one vote and in practice decisions are adopted by consensus, even if officially decisions may be adopted by a majority vote. COPs can only adopt decisions that legally bind the parties to the MEA if the MEA or a protocol explicitly so determines. Such an explicit determination is exceptional. The procedure incorporated in the Montreal Protocol for adopting further reductions or phasing out decisions regarding ozone-depleting substances is the often referred to example. Article 2(9) of the Protocol provides that these types of decisions, if consensus cannot be obtained, can be adopted by a two-third majority of the parties present and voting and will be binding for all parties to the Protocol. However, in practice these decisions have been adopted by consensus. Other MEAs which provide for majority decision-making processes for amending regulations, for example the listing of protected species or banned substances, usually also provide a so-called opting-out procedure by way of which a state party may inform the secretariat that it does not wish to be bound by the amendment. Opting-out procedures are part of, for example, the procedure for amending CITES' annexes of listed species (Art. XV(1)(b)and (c) and (3)) and the procedure for adopting a new annex or amending the annexes to the Rotterdam Convention, with the exception of Annex III, which lists the chemicals subject to the prior informed consent procedure (Art. 22). In the latter case the consensus-based procedure outlined in section 3.5.1 applies.

COPs and their decision-making processes do not stand in isolation. Their task is supported by the work of subsidiary bodies of a permanent or ad hoc character, as well as by institutions outside the regime but that are linked to it. Most MEAs establish a permanent body that provides advice on scientific and technical issues. The Subsidiary Body on Scientific, Technical and Technological Advice under the Biodiversity Convention provides an example. Subsidiary bodies prepare most COP decisions and some subsidiary bodies are responsible for implementing parts of an international environmental regime. An example of the former type of body is the CITES Standing Committee, a body of limited composition, which oversees the activities of the secretariat and other subsidiary bodies during the inter-sessional period between COPs and, among other tasks, prepares decisions for the COP. An example of the latter type of body is the CDM's Executive Board. It is the body responsible for the implementation of the flexible mechanism, the CDM, established by Article 12 of the Kyoto Protocol, which allows developed states to invest in emission reductions of GHGs in developing states and use those emissions to meet their obligations under the Protocol. It is a body of limited composition which, among other things, determines the standards for the validation of CDM projects. Another example of a body that implements an MEA is the World Heritage Committee established by the World Heritage Convention (Art. 8(1)). It is a body of limited composition that decides on the listing of heritage sites, including natural heritage sites, and develops the criteria for such listing (Art. 11). In addition, the committee also keeps a "list of World Heritage in Danger" (Art. 11(4)). IUCN advises the World Heritage Committee on the listing of natural heritage sites (Art. 8(3); also see Art. 14(2)).

IUCN's link to the world heritage regime provides an example of an institution that is not established by the regime, but that nevertheless plays an important role in it. Another salient example of such an institution is the IPCC. It was established in 1988 by the WMO and UNEP and through a peer-review procedure provides expert advice on all aspects of climate change and response strategies. The work of the IPCC provided an important impetus for the adoption of the UNFCCC and has continued to provide input for the climate change negotiations and for the development of responses to climate change.

Despite the fact that COP decisions or the decisions of subsidiary organs generally are not legally binding, they can significantly affect the rights and duties of a party under the treaty as well as the interests of private sector actors. For example, the CMP of the Kyoto Protocol has adopted decisions that determine the conditions under which a party and private actors linked to that party may participate in the flexible mechanisms established by the Protocol. For CDM projects one of these conditions is additionality (Art. 12(5)(c), Protocol), entailing that investments in a CDM project must provide reductions of GHGs additional to those that would have been obtained in the absence of the CDM investment (section 5.5). The level of additionality of a project ultimately co-determines the emission reduction units that a project generates. Guidance on how to set the baselines for determining additionality, among a host of other things, are set out in a decision of the CMP (Dec. 3/CMP.1); other decisions of the CMP have been further developed in practices of the CDM's Executive Board. These decisions and practices together thus co-determine the potential return on investment, in terms of emission reduction units, that a project is likely to generate and an investor to obtain. The CMP thereby engages in normative development and when the CDM's Executive Board applies these guidelines to projects it engages in executive decision-making.

Decisions taken by the World Heritage Committee to list a site, which requires the approval of the state concerned, may also have far reaching effects, including for private actors. In Australia's Kakadu National Park listing reportedly halted a planned mining activity and in its Wet Tropics of Queensland site stopped logging but boosted tourism. In relation to Kakadu National Park it is of interest to note that the Mirarr People, the traditional custodians of the land, have on various occasions sent a delegation to UNESCO headquarters in Paris. The Mirarr People's trips to UNESCO illustrate how the local and the global are intimately related.

Another example of a way in which legally non-binding decisions adopted within an MEA may influence the rights and duties of states parties as well as private sector actors is provided by notifications which the CITES secretariat regularly issues. CITES' Notification to the Parties No. 2014/017 on missing and verification of permits from the Democratic Republic of Congo (DRC) recommended that parties not accept export permits or certificates apparently issued in the DRC. Now assume that a trader in CITES specimens in good faith has relied on a permit from the DRC, but that this permit is not recognized as valid by the Netherlands, the state of import, based on European Union legislation[1] related to CITES in conjunction with the notification. Can the private trader successfully argue that EU legislation itself does not prohibit or caution against trade in CITES specimens from the DRC and that the notification does not offer a valid title for rejecting the permit, since it is not legally binding, and that therefore the Netherlands should allow the import to proceed? May be not, since in *Commission v. France* (Case C-182/89) the European Court of Justice ruled that France should have acted exactly as the Netherlands did in the above-mentioned example based in this case on EU legislation and a legally non-binding CITES COP-resolution, concerning the dire state of implementation of the Convention in Bolivia. As such a legally non-binding decision may thus obtain legal significance if a court is able and willing to link it to relevant local law, in this case the EU-CITES Regulation.

The institutional structure provided by most MEAs that require decision-making at the global level also includes a financial mechanism which serves to assist developing states in implementing the MEA. The discussion of these mechanisms is included in section 5.5, as it

---

1 Regulation (EC) No. 338/97 (EU-CITES Regulation).

provides a particular way in which MEAs are linked to international organizations. In addition, many MEAs that require decision-making at the global level establish compliance mechanisms. These bodies serve to verify implementation of relevant decisions and do so in a non-confrontational way. Compliance mechanisms are discussed in section 6.3.

5.4   Institutional linkages

MEAs are linked in a variety of ways. One of the most prominent links is the overlap between their mandates. For example, the protection of forests will serve biodiversity but also help to mitigate climate change by reducing GHGs in the atmosphere and reduce the effects of climate change by preventing flooding and landslides. Similarly, protecting mangroves along the coast in order to prevent flooding due to sea-level rise linked to climate change, also referred to as ecosystem-based adaptation, is also likely to enhance biodiversity. An international watercourse may be the topic of a watercourse agreement, part of it may be a wetland designated under the Ramsar Convention and that same part or others may be listed as a natural heritage site under the World Heritage Convention. The watercourse, moreover, may harbour migratory species protected under the Bonn Convention and listed under CITES. These linkages between the substantive matters regulated by way of different MEAs are often referred to as synergies, meaning that action taken to address one problem will also serve to address other problems and thus serve to implement a number of MEAs. The need to identify and work on these synergies has led to climate change now being a topic on the agenda of most MEAs and to initiatives to institutionalize links between MEAs. An example of such an initiative is the Joint Liaison Group in which the Biodiversity Convention, the UNFCCC and 1994 Desertification Convention participate with the aim of foregrounding the synergies between the three conventions. The integration of the secretariats of and further identification of synergies between the Basel, Stockholm and Rotterdam conventions provides another example. However, as has been suggested, much can be improved in this respect.

In terms of normative development, a noteworthy link is the one between the LOS Convention and IMO regulations that enhance maritime safety or protection of the marine environment. The LOS Convention in numerous of its provisions regarding the safety of navigation (Art. 22(3)(a)) and the prevention of vessel source pollution (Art. 211(2)) refers to the "recommendations of the competent international organization" or "generally accepted international rules and standards established through the competent international organization or general diplomatic conference". These provisions are generally understood to refer to the IMO or a diplomatic conference at which a new agreement is adopted related to the safety of navigation or the prevention of marine pollution, likely to be organized by the IMO. As mentioned above, these provisions thereby determine that vessel source pollution is to be regulated by the IMO and thus by global decision-making. However, these provisions also result in recommendations and generally accepted international rules and standards being incorporated into the LOS Convention by way of referencing and thereby attaining normative relevance for all parties to the LOS Convention, also those that might not be parties to or participating in normative development at the IMO.

Many MEAs are institutionally linked to international organizations because their secretariats are administered by international organizations. These secretariats are located in various countries and linked to a variety of United Nations institutions, even if some also operate independently. UNEP, with headquarters in Nairobi, Kenya, administers the secretariat of CITES, located in Geneva, Switzerland; the secretariat of the Vienna Convention on the Ozone Layer and its Montreal Protocol, located in Nairobi, Kenya; the secretariat of the Biodiversity Convention and its two protocols, located in Montreal, Canada; and the secretariat of the Bonn Convention, located in Bonn, Germany. The joint secretariats of the Basel, Stockholm and Rotterdam Conventions are also administered by UNEP and located in Geneva, Switzerland, even if part of the secretariat of the Rotterdam Convention, as related to pesticides, is administered by the FAO and located in Rome, Italy. The secretariats of the UNFCCC and Kyoto Protocol, as well as the secretariat of Desertification Convention, are administered by the United Nations and located in Bonn, Germany. The IMO, located in London, United Kingdom, administers the secretariats of global treaties related to shipping, such as the MARPOL Convention, and also the London Convention. Whereas the IAEA, located in Vienna, Austria, administers the secretariats for many conventions related to the use of nuclear material; with the OECD in Paris, France, administering others. The secretariat of the IWC, located in Cambridge, United Kingdom, is an example of an independent institution. The secretariat of the Ramsar Convention is also independent, even if its staff are legally IUCN staff and it shares its premises with the IUCN office in Gland, Switzerland. The secretariat of the World Heritage Convention is administered by UNESCO, located in Paris, France. Lastly, the LOS Convention and the Fish Stocks Agreement are administered by the Division for Ocean Affairs and the Law of the Sea at United Nations Headquarters in New York, United States, while the other MEA on fisheries, the 1993 FAO Compliance Agreement, is administered by the FAO. This patchwork of institutions located at various places in the world can be explained historically; however, it shall come as no surprise that it is regularly regarded as one of the barriers that would need to be addressed if the synergies between MEAs are to be improved.

MEAs are also linked to international organizations because the latter execute projects on the ground that implement MEAs in developing states. These links may find their origin in a developed state or group of developed states financing a project that serves to implement an MEA in a developing state. The "Ecosystem Based Adaptation in Mountain Ecosystems" project implemented in Nepal, Peru and Uganda provides an example of the former. The project is financed by the German government, coordinated by UNEP and implemented jointly by UNEP, UNDP and IUCN, and serves to implement in particular the UNFCCC. In addition, scientific bodies such as the IPPC and GESAMP, which are themselves cooperative efforts established by international organizations, also link in to the work of MEAs.

In terms of institutional patterns another link is prominent in international environmental law. This is the link between MEA-based financial mechanisms, special funds, international financial institutions and other international organizations implementing projects on the ground. These links will be discussed in the next section.

5.5   MEAs, financial mechanisms and international financial institutions

As mentioned, most MEAs explicitly provide for financial mechanisms; this is especially true for those MEAs adopted at or after the Rio Conference. These mechanisms serve to implement the commitment of developed states to transfer funds and technical know-how to developing states for purposes of implementing the MEA in question. Financial mechanisms typically finance the so-called incremental costs of a project. These are the costs associated with turning a project or activity into a more environmentally friendly one with global benefits, also referred to as the additionality of a project (section 5.3). Examples of how global benefits may be obtained, and thus incremental costs identified, are turning a coal-fired energy plant into one using natural gas and thus reducing the emission of GHGs or realizing a change in logging methods with the aim of protecting biodiversity.

The existence of financial mechanisms does not imply that bilateral aid or mechanisms outside the MEA-based financial mechanisms do not play a role in implementing those commitments. They do and all means of financing exist side by side, as the German financed "Ecosystem Based Adaptation in Mountain Ecosystems", referred to above illustrates (section 5.4). KAZA, discussed in section 2.3, provides another example, as do projects financed by regional development banks such as the Asian Development Bank.

Examples of provisions in MEAs which concern the establishment of financial mechanisms are Article 10 of the Montreal Protocol and Article 11 of the UNFCCC. Based on these types of provisions, MEAs have themselves established funds and have designated funds established within the World Bank as financial mechanisms.

Relevant funds that are administered within the climate change regime are the Green Climate Fund and the Adaptation Fund. The Ramsar Convention is an example of a convention that initially did not have a financial mechanism. However, in 1990 the Small Grants Fund, then called the Wetland Conservation Fund, was established to assist developing states and states with economies in transition in the conservation and wise use of wetlands. The Fund is administered by the secretariat under the supervision of the Ramsar Standing Committee. Contributions to the Fund are voluntary and have come from states as well as the private sector. The beneficiaries of the Small Grants Fund can be an agency, an NGO or an individual, subject to the condition that the Ramsar implementing agency in the government of the state where the project will be executed endorses and monitors the project. The Bonn Convention operates a similar Small Grants Fund as do some of the cooperative arrangements concluded under the auspices of the Bonn Convention (section 5.2.2). The Fish Stocks Agreement also operates its own fund, known as the Assistance Fund. It finances efforts to implement the agreement in developing states and in particular in least developed states. The Fund was established on the basis of an UNGA resolution, is administered by the FAO and considers applications from developing states parties to the Fish Stocks Agreement (Res. A/58/14 and Terms of Ref.). While the Assistance Fund may receive donations from different types of actors, between 2004 until the end of 2012, only seven states had contributed to the Fund. The World Heritage Convention also operates its own fund, administered by UNESCO (Art. 15). The Montreal Protocol similarly administers its own fund, known as the Multilateral Fund, with its secretariat located in Montreal, Canada. The Multilateral Fund is financed by developed states parties to the Montreal Protocol, but may also receive contributions from non-governmental sources. Implementing agencies of the Multilateral Fund are the World Bank, UNDP, UNEP and the United Nations Industrial Development Organization (UNIDO). These organizations thereby serve to develop and execute projects, financed by the Multilateral Fund, in developing and economy in transition states.

The GEF is the institution by way of which the World Bank, together with UNEP and UNDP and on the basis of the guidance provided by a number of COPs, shapes the financial mechanisms of a number of MEAs. The GEF was established first in 1991 as a pilot project by the World Bank; it attained its present structure in 1994 after significant reform. This reform became necessary when developing states would not accept the GEF as the financial mechanism for the Biodiversity Convention and the UNFCCC, due to the fact that it was controlled solely by the World Bank (section 2.4). The main changes that were introduced in 1994 are as follows. First, receivers of GEF funding, developing states and economy in transition states, and donors, developed states, were given an equal say in the GEF. Second, de facto the GEF was now established by the World Bank together with UNEP and UNDP, even if de jure it remains a subsidiary body of the World Bank because UNEP and UNDP, as programmes of the UNGA, cannot establish subsidiary bodies of this nature. The World Bank is the administrator of the GEF Trust Fund and represents the GEF when de jure representation is required, such as in signing the agreements between MEAs and the GEF (para. 27, GEF Instrument and para. 7, Annex B to the GEF Instrument). The latter implies that the GEF does not have legal personality under international law. The GEF functions as the financial mechanism for the UNFCCC, the Biodiversity Convention, the Desertification Convention, the Stockholm Convention and the Minamata Convention as well as protocols related to these conventions. In addition, the GEF funds projects related to the reduction and phasing out of ozone-depleting substances, the protection of international waters, both oceans and watercourses, and sustainable forestry.

A large number of organizations function as GEF Agencies which, as the implementing agencies of the Multilateral Fund, develop project proposals and manage GEF-funded projects in developing states and states with economies in transition. In July 2015, GEF Agencies included the Asian Development Bank, the African Development Bank, the Development Bank of Southern Africa, Conservation International, the European Bank for Reconstruction and Development (EBRD), the FAO, the Inter-American Development Bank (IADB), the International Fund for Agricultural Development, IUCN, UNDP, UNEP, UNIDO, the World Bank and WWF. Noteworthy about this list are two elements, in particular. First, that NGOs – Conservation International, IUCN and WWF – act as GEF Agencies. Second, development banks, both regional and the World Bank, are heavily involved in the GEF and thus in executing MEA-related projects, also in relation to those MEAs for which the GEF is not the official financial mechanism, such as the Watercourses Convention.

The GEF also administers a number of special funds that were established by the COPs of MEAs. These funds include the Nagoya Protocol Implementation Fund established within the biodiversity regime and the Least Developed Countries Fund and Special Climate Change Fund established within the climate change regime. The GEF also provides secretarial services to the Adaptation Fund, established under the Kyoto Protocol, which is financed by way of a 2 per cent levy on the CERs generated from CDM projects.

In addition, the World Bank acts as the trustee for the Green Climate Fund, established under the UNFCCC. The World Bank moreover administers a number of climate funds on behalf of states, including "Netherlands CDM Facility" and "Netherlands European Carbon Facility". It has also established international funds, such as the PCF. Both public and private actors contribute to the PCF, which invests in GHG reduction projects and in return receives certified emission reduction units. Certified emission reduction units can be traded on the carbon market and used to meet a developed state's emission reduction units under the Kyoto Protocol. Interestingly, while at the time of writing the climate negotiations were in an uncertain phase, the World Bank was already experimenting with new types of facilities, such as the Carbon Partnership Facility, for the post-Kyoto period. Perhaps this is the clearest sign that the flexible mechanisms will be part of a successor to the Kyoto Protocol (section 3.4.3).

The commitment to transfer funds from developed to developing states, and related thereto the establishment of financial mechanisms, is one of the means by which the principle of common but differentiated responsibilities has been implemented in international environmental law (section 4.5.7). As the above description illustrates, international financial institutions, developing banks in particular and the World Bank most in particular, play an important role in implementing that commitment. It might be argued that developed states have outsourced part of their commitment to transfer finances and know-how to these institutions, which are as a result able to exercise considerable public power in developing states and states with economies in transition.

5.6   Assessment

The institutional structures of international environmental law are complex and have been criticized for being disjointed. This is not entirely surprising given that complex interdependencies of a socioeconomic nature are involved, entailing that different actors frame their interests in distinct ways. Add thereto the relatively recent beginnings of contemporary international environmental law in the 1970s, and it becomes clear that room for experimentation was required. The variety of institutions so far established certainly offers that room, and, as many have argued, institutional streamlining now seems to make sense.

Are there drawbacks to such institutional diversity? Yes there are and they concern, among other things, differences of opinion about the competences of institutions involved. Such a difference of opinion plays a role in determining whether the dismantling of ships should be addressed solely by way of the Hong Kong Convention or whether the Basel Convention is also competent (section 3.5.3). Similar discussions played a role in determining whether GHG emissions from ships and aircraft should be dealt with by way of the climate change regime or by the United Nations specialized agency for shipping, the IMO, and for air traffic, the International Civil Aviation Organization. In addition, discussions continue to surface whether it is appropriate to list commercially fished stocks that are in danger of depletion or marine mammals on CITES annexes or whether they should only be regulated by, respectively, RFMOs and bodies that specifically seek to protect marine mammals, such as the IWC. While these discussions at first sight are primarily about the competences of international institutions, they also involve, and perhaps primarily relate to, the competences of national institutions. For example, if the dismantling of ships is regulated under the auspices of the IMO, the organization under whose auspices the Hong Kong Convention was developed, government offices responsible for shipping, often with strong links to the shipping industry, are likely to have a significant impact. If the same topic is addressed by the Basel Convention, government offices responsible for environmental protection tend to have the lead. Similarly, commercial fisheries tend to be the responsibility of government offices with strong links to the fishing sector, but if a topic is regulated by CITES, government offices dealing with nature protection or environmental protection are likely to have the lead. "Turf fights" among international bodies are probably inevitable, but it is important to realize that their origin can be linked to how responsibilities are allocated at the national level.

While turf fights might be inevitable, coordination and cooperation within this complex institutional system is important, also because resources are scarce. Yet, significant coordination is taking place, at least in some respects. This coordination is engaged in by the World Bank and the funds and implementing agencies associated with the Bank. However, this coordination is one-sided, it concerns the implementation of MEAs in developing states, in particular. As a result, the World Bank, together with other actors, is exerting significant public powers in developing states with the objective of attaining sustainable development. This is probably not what developing states were aiming for when they started their quest for a reframing of environmental problems as socio-economic problems and reform of international institutions in preparation for the 1972 Stockholm Conference (section 2.4).

Developing states, then, have been successful in influencing the reconceptualization of environmental problems as socio-economic problems, a reconceptualization that seems to have been embraced by developed states. This reconceptualization, however, seems to have come at a price. Namely, the enhanced influence of international organizations, the World Bank in particular, in developing states. It might also be argued that the promise of justice inherent in international environmental law principles (Chapter 4), especially those that concern relations of interdependence between developing and developed states (section 4.5), is compromised by some of the institutional structures that are part of international environmental law.

6 Dispute settlement and accountability mechanisms

6.1 Introduction

The general rules of international law applicable to inter-state dispute settlement apply to inter-state environmental disputes. That is, Article 33 of the United Nations Charter applies. It requires states to settle their disputes "by negotiation, enquiry, mediation, conciliation, arbitration, judicial settlement, resort to regional agencies or arrangements, or other peaceful means of their own choice". This means that states are bound to settle their disputes peacefully, but that they are free to use a procedure of their own choice to attain this end. It also means that states are not bound to settle their dispute by judicial means, in other words, via international courts or tribunals, including arbitral tribunals. In order for an international court or tribunal to have jurisdiction in a specific dispute the states parties to that dispute will have had to consent to the court or tribunal exercising its jurisdiction. It is generally agreed that states are reluctant to submit their disputes to judicial settlement procedures, probably because compared to other procedures for dispute settlement, the control that parties have over the outcome of the procedure is limited.

In case of disputes involving international environmental law, inter-state judicial procedures for the settlement of disputes present a number of drawbacks. First, these procedures tend to take place after the environmental damage has occurred. Second, inter-state judicial procedures tend to be confrontational whereas environmental degradation and unsustainable development, especially if linked to lack of technology and know-how or financial resources, may be better addressed through dialogue and cooperation. Third, important actors in the development and implementation of international environmental law, such as international financial organizations (section 5.5), cannot participate in inter-state judicial procedures. Fourth, individuals and groups in society undergo the consequences of unsustainable development and environmental degradation, yet they do not have access to inter-state judicial dispute settlement procedures. Fifth, many environmental disputes involve multiple actors, including private sector actors and these actors, as international organizations and individuals and groups in society, do not have access to inter-state dispute settlement procedures. It is these considerations that have given rise to the establishment of alternative procedures for dealing with international environmental disputes and for addressing non-compliance with applicable standards or regulations.

Four developments can be distinguished in contemporary international environmental law which seek to address the drawbacks of inter-state dispute settlement procedures. First, many more recently adopted MEAs require states to engage in compulsory conciliation, at the request of any party to the dispute if they cannot settle their disputes by other means. Second, state-triggered non-confrontational compliance procedures are now part of most MEAs, with a few compliance mechanisms allocating a role to a third party. Third, procedures that allow an individual or group in society to complain about non-compliance with applicable standards have been established by IDBs but also by the Aarhus Convention. Fourth, private parties have established complaint mechanisms. In addition, dispute settlement procedures available in other areas of international law, such as human rights law, international trade law and international investment law are relevant to international environmental law. These latter procedures are discussed in Chapter 7. This chapter first discusses the provisions of MEAs on inter-state dispute settlement. It then considers MEA-based compliance mechanisms that may be triggered by states or a third party and subsequently examines compliance mechanisms that can be triggered by individuals and groups in society, including those established by private actors.

6.2   MEAs and inter-state dispute settlement procedures

Older MEAs generally provide that disputes between the parties shall be addressed by negotiations. If the dispute is not resolved through negotiations, these agreements provide that the parties, if they agree, may choose to submit the dispute to arbitration, at the Permanent Court of Arbitration (PCA) or according to an arbitration procedure provided for in an Annex to the MEA in question. CITES (Art. 28) and the Bonn Convention (Art. 13) are examples of treaties that refer to the PCA; MARPOL is an example of an MEA that itself provides an arbitration procedure (Art. 10, Protocol II). These types of procedures basically incorporate the general rule provided in Article 33 of the United Nations Charter into the MEA in question. The legal implications of these MEAs' provisions on dispute settlement, then, do not go beyond those of agreements that do not contain provisions on dispute settlement, such as the Ramsar Convention and the International Whaling Convention. In these latter cases, Article 33 of the United Nations Charter remains applicable. This means that in case of CITES, the Bonn Convention, the Ramsar Convention and the International Whaling Convention the applicable rule is as follows: disputes are to be settled peacefully and only if the states involved in the dispute agree will those disputes be submitted to a judicial dispute settlement procedure.

The Notification Convention (Art. 11) and the Assistance Convention (Art. 13), both relating to nuclear accidents, are examples of another type of inter-state dispute settlement provision in an MEA. They provide for negotiations or any other peaceful means of settling the dispute and if that process leads to no result then, as a second step, any party to the dispute may submit it to arbitration or the ICJ. However, upon signing, ratifying, accepting or acceding to these conventions, states may opt-out of the second step in the procedure. Many states parties to these conventions have availed themselves of this option, as a result exempting most inter-state disputes from compulsory judicial settlement procedures. These same conventions also recognize that disputes between a state and the Agency, the IAEA, may arise. These disputes, however, are subject only to the rule that requires parties to negotiate or use any other agreed peaceful means to settle the dispute. Again, such disputes will not be the subject of judicial dispute settlement procedures, unless the parties to the dispute agree thereto.

Many MEAs concluded after the 1992 Rio Conference require their parties to settle disputes by negotiations or any other peaceful means of their own choice and determine that if this process does not lead to a settlement within a certain period of time the dispute be submitted to conciliation or fact-finding at the request of any of the parties to the dispute. These MEAs thereby provide for a compulsory process, fact-finding or conciliation, that states have to engage in if one of them so requests, even if the outcome of that process will not be legally binding. Many of these MEAs also give states the option of declaring that they will accept, with respect to another party accepting the same process, the jurisdiction of an arbitral tribunal or of the ICJ. MEAs which incorporate this three-step approach to dispute settlement – negotiations, compulsory conciliation and the option of judicial settlement – include the UNFCCC (Art. 14), the Biodiversity Convention (Art. 27), the Rotterdam Convention (Art. 20), the Stockholm Convention (Art. 18), the Watercourses Convention (Art. 33) and the Minamata Convention (Art. 25). Very few states parties to these MEAs, however, have chosen to accept the available judicial settlement procedures. In addition, to the best of this author's knowledge the conciliation procedures available under these MEAs have not been used.

The LOS Convention, in Part XV, contains a complicated system of dispute settlement, which also applies to the Fish Stocks Agreement (Art. 30). It provides for a number of compulsory judicial dispute settlement procedures which states may opt for when ratifying the Convention, including the ICJ, ITLOS, and several forms of arbitration. If two states involved in a dispute have chosen different means of dispute settlement then the arbitral procedure as set out in Annex VII of the Convention applies (Art. 287). The LOS Convention also provides that disputes regarding the exercise of coastal state jurisdiction in its EEZ will only under certain circumstances be subject to judicial dispute settlement procedures, with some of the excluded disputes regarding fisheries being subject to compulsory conciliation (Art. 297). This means that the framing of a dispute concerning fisheries or the protection of the marine environment is important, as it determines which dispute settlement procedure applies.

The judicial dispute settlement procedures reviewed in this section have been used infrequently and if used have not in all cases resulted in a decision on the merits. The *MOX Plant* case, brought by Ireland against the United Kingdom, the *Southern Bluefin Tuna* cases, brought by Australia and New Zealand against Japan, the case *Concerning Land Reclamation by Singapore in and around the Strait of Johor*, brought by Malaysia against Singapore, and the *Arctic Sunrise* case, brought by the Netherlands against Russia, are arbitration procedures based on Annex VII of the LOS Convention and came before ITLOS for the determination of provisional measures (Art. 290). The *Arctic Sunrise* arbitration was decided on the merits through the PCA with the arbitral tribunal awarding damages to the Netherlands and ordering Russia to return all persons and confiscated materials to the Netherlands, to the extent this had not been done already. However, none of the other cases were decided on the merits. In 2000, an International Centre for the Settlement of Investment Disputes (ICSID) arbitral tribunal in the *Southern Bluefin Tuna* cases found it lacked jurisdiction. In 2003, the *MOX Plant* case, pending at the PCA, was terminated when it emerged that Ireland had brought the case in conflict with its obligation under European Union law to submit disputes involving European Union law to the European Union Court of Justice. The case *Concerning Land Reclamation by Singapore in and around the Strait of Johor* was settled by negotiation, even if the PCA arbitral tribunal issued an award on agreed terms in 2005.

Other recently decided inter-state cases came before the ICJ or an arbitral tribunal based on general rules of international law, as opposed to rules of international environmental law. The *Pulp Mills* case, brought by Argentina against Uruguay, was based on a provision in the River Uruguay Statute that attributes jurisdiction to the ICJ. The ICJ was able to exercise jurisdiction in the case concerning *Whaling in the Antarctic*, brought by Australia against Japan with New Zealand intervening, because Australia and Japan had both made declarations recognizing the jurisdiction of the Court based on Article 36(2) of the Statute of the ICJ.[1] The *Gabčíkovo-Nagymaros* case was brought before the ICJ based on a special agreement concluded between Hungary and Slovakia. Similarly, the arbitral tribunal's jurisdiction in the *Iron Rhine* arbitration was based on a special agreement concluded between Belgium and the Netherlands.

The above suggests that also in disputes concerning international environmental law states remain reluctant to use available inter-state judicial procedures. Alternatively, it might be argued that these procedures are not well suited to resolve many of the issues at stake, which ultimately require interaction, negotiation and compromise between the states concerned. In fact, one of the outcomes of most of the rulings referred to above is that the states concerned should engage in negotiations in order to address the problems at stake.

6.3   MEAs and compliance mechanisms

Most recently adopted MEAs or their protocols include a provision that directs the states parties to establish a compliance mechanism.

---

1 Note that Japan changed it declaration recognizing the jurisdiction of the ICJ with the aim of excluding disputes involving marine living resources, including whales, from the jurisdiction of the ICJ on 5 October 2015.

These provisions typically are part of the instrument in the regime that contains concrete obligations for their states parties. In the cases of the Basel, Stockholm, Rotterdam and Minamata Conventions, these provisions are part of the original MEA; while in the cases of the ozone, climate change and biodiversity regimes they are part of the protocols adopted within those regimes. Compliance mechanisms have been established for the Basel Convention, the Montreal Protocol, the Kyoto Protocol, the Cartagena Protocol and the Nagoya Protocol. The establishment of a compliance mechanism is being considered for the Stockholm and Rotterdam Conventions. Given that the Minamata Convention has only recently been adopted and not entered into force, its compliance mechanism has not been developed. Inter-state compliance mechanisms tend to have the same structure, with the Kyoto Protocol compliance mechanism being the exception. The Kyoto Protocol compliance committee consists of a facilitative and an enforcement branch, with the two branches constituting the compliance committee, and the enforcement branch being subject to more stringent procedures given the potential consequences of its findings.

Compliance committees, and under the Montreal Protocol the Implementation Committee, are subsidiary bodies of the main plenary body; they have a limited number of members, often 15, who are elected by the main plenary body based on their capacity and equitable geographical representation, with some procedures also requiring that members shall act in their personal capacity. The Nagoya Protocol compliance committee, in addition to its 15 members, also consists of two observers representing indigenous and local communities. These observers may participate in deliberations but not in decision-making and also otherwise have more limited rights than the members of the compliance committee (Decision NP 1/4, 2014). Members of a compliance committee serve for limited terms, normally in the order of five years and often with the option of serving for two terms.

Compliance mechanisms serve to assess compliance with the instrument in question; do so in a non-confrontational manner and their findings are legally non-binding. Compliance committees usually have two distinct tasks: assessing general issues of compliance and reviewing specific situations in which an allegation of non-compliance has been submitted to it. The former task typically involves the review of reports submitted by states and assessing these in terms of compliance with the obligations under the relevant convention or protocol. The second task involves considering allegations of non-compliance submitted to it by a state party regarding its own compliance or a state party regarding the compliance of another state party. Some compliance procedures, including those under the Basel Convention and Montreal Protocol, also allow the secretariat to submit allegations of non-compliance and the Kyoto Protocol allows submissions through the secretariat of questions that expert review teams raise in their reports concerning a party's compliance. The Nagoya Protocol compliance committee, furthermore, "may examine systemic issues of general non-compliance that come to its attention" (para. D.11, Decision NP 1/4, 2014). It will be interesting to see how this phrase will be interpreted by the committee. Will it consider an allegation of systemic non-compliance brought to its attention by an individual or group in society or only those brought to its attention by the secretariat?

If a compliance committee finds non-compliance it will recommend measures that a state party should take to improve compliance and, in case of a developing state or an economy in transition state, recommend that steps be taken to facilitate financial or technical assistance. In some cases, such as the Basel Convention and the Montreal Protocol, the compliance committee may recommend that the COP adopt additional measures against a state in non-compliance, such as the issuing of a caution.

The compliance mechanism under the Kyoto Protocol follows the general pattern outlined above for its facilitative branch. This compliance mechanism, however, is more elaborate in that it also consists of an enforcement branch. The enforcement branch considers allegations of non-compliance regarding the specific emission reduction obligations that rest on Annex I states, their reporting requirements and their eligibility to participate in the flexible mechanisms. In other words, it takes decisions that concern the core of the obligations of the Kyoto Protocol. If a state party is found to be in non-compliance by the enforcement branch it will be required to develop a plan for remedying the situation, to be reviewed by the enforcement branch, which will also review the implementation of the plan. In addition, the enforcement branch will also suspend a state party's right to participate in emissions trading. Given these far reaching consequences the procedure also provides for an appeal procedure with the CMP, if the state concerned finds that it was denied due process by the enforcement branch. Due to its considerable powers, it seems highly unlikely that an institution such as the enforcement branch of the Kyoto Protocol compliance mechanism will be part of its successor.

By July 2015 the Basel Convention compliance mechanism had considered two self-submissions and 12 submissions from the secretariat; the COP of the Montreal Protocol, based on the work of the Implementation Committee, had taken over 70 decisions regarding non-compliance; the enforcement branch of the Kyoto Protocol compliance mechanism had considered eight situations of non-compliance, all of which arose from the work of expert review teams, and the facilitative branch has received 15 complaints of non-compliance from the chair of the Group of 77 concerning non-timely submission of certain data by Annex I parties. By July 2015, the compliance mechanisms for the Cartagena and Nagoya Protocols had not received any complaints of non-compliance.

Compliance procedures have also become part of the institutional structure of older conventions. Relevant examples include CITES (Resolution 14.3, 2007) and the London Convention (LC 19/17, Annex 7, 2007), while the Bonn Convention, at its eleventh COP held in November 2014, decided to consider establishing a review mechanism (UNEP/CMS/Resolution 11.7). The compliance procedure of the London Convention can only be triggered by states. By July 2015, the London Convention compliance mechanism had not received complaints of non-compliance.

The CITES compliance procedures are different from other compliance mechanisms. Both substantively and institutionally they constitute a compilation of procedures that were already in place in CITES, now known as the CITES compliance procedures (Res. Conf. 14.3). These procedures do not create an additional body but work through the main CITES Bodies – the COP, Standing Committee, the Animals Committee and the Plants Committee – which already provided a rather comprehensive process for identifying, monitoring and making public, through notifications, problems of non-compliance with the convention (section 5.3). Within CITES the secretariat triggers the procedure, based on information that it receives. CITES regularly issues recommendations to suspend trade with specific states, based on its compliance procedures.

In addition to the procedures in global environmental regimes, at the regional level the UNECE conventions, such as the Espoo Convention, also provide for compliance mechanisms. Most of these can only be triggered by states. The Aarhus Convention and its 2003 protocol on pollutant release and transfer registers (PRTR Protocol), are the exception: their compliance mechanisms can also be triggered by individuals or groups (section 6.4.2).

In practice, with a few exceptions, allegations of non-compliance reach compliance committees not because states trigger them in respect of their own compliance or those of other parties to the instrument, but because a third party – secretariats under CITES and the Montreal Protocol or under the Kyoto Protocol an expert review team – identifies issues of non-compliance. It is thus understandable that the Cartagena Protocol and London Convention compliance mechanisms, which do not allow the secretariat or a third party to submit allegations of non-compliance, have, to date, not received any allegations of non-compliance and have instead focused on general issues of compliance only.

6.4   Individual or group triggered accountability mechanisms

There are several procedures available in international instruments related to the environment that allow individuals or groups in society to submit allegations of non-compliance. These include the procedures available at IDBs, the above-mentioned Aarhus Convention Compliance Committee (ACCC) and procedures developed by private actors. Each of these types of procedure is discussed below.

6.4.1   International development banks

Most IDBs have established accountability mechanisms, also referred to as grievance mechanisms, before which an individual, two or more individuals or groups in society can bring complaints. In 1993, the World Bank established the first of these mechanisms. At that time, the Executive Boards of the International Bank for Reconstruction and Development (IBRD) and the International Development Agency (IDA) adopted identical resolutions establishing the World Bank Inspection Panel (WBIP). Since then other IDBs have followed suit:

- In 1994, the IADB established the Independent Investigation Mechanism and in February 2010 its successor, the Independent Consultation and Investigation Mechanism.
- In 1999, the International Finance Corporation (IFC) and the Multilateral Investment Guarantee Agency (MIGA) established the office of the Compliance Advisor/Ombudsman (CAO).

- In 1995 the Asian Development Bank established the Inspection Function and in 2003 its successor, the Asian Development Bank Accountability Mechanism, which was significantly revised in 2012.
- In 2004, the EBRD established the Independent Recourse Mechanism and in May 2009 its successor, the Project Compliant Mechanism.
- In 2006, the African Development Bank established the Independent Review Mechanism.

The mandates of IDB accountability mechanisms are similar but not identical. All IDB accountability mechanisms consider complaints by individuals or groups in society, including NGOs. In general terms, a complaint should concern the following: that the complainants rights or interests are being or are likely to be harmed by an act or omission of the IDB as a result of the IDB failing to implement its own OP&Ps, for example, regarding EIA (section 4.7.4), in regards of a project financed by the IDB. The complaint thus is directed against the IDB and not against the beneficiary of the loan, usually a state or, in case of the IFC and MIGA, a company. At the end of the procedure, IDB accountability mechanisms submit recommendations to the executive body of the IDB in question, instead of to the IDBs' management bodies who are involved in the design and implementation of projects and the object of the compliant. The recommendatory character of the outcome of IDB accountability procedures implies that they are not legally binding.

Two important differences between the mandates of IDB accountability mechanisms concern the following. First, whether the mechanism is entitled to engage only in compliance review or also in problem-solving. All IDB accountability mechanisms, except for the WBIP, are explicitly mandated to engage in problem-solving. The WBIP, however, in recent years, based on the experience of other IDB accountability mechanisms, informally has introduced problem-solving during the phase in which it examines the eligibility of a complaint. Second, some IDB accountability mechanisms may not consider complaints by single individuals; while all may consider complaints by groups. A single individual may submit a complaint to, for example, the IADB's Independent Consultation and Investigation Mechanism and the EBRD's Project Compliant Mechanism and the IFC/MIGAs CAO. The WBIP, the Asian Development Bank Accountability Mechanism and the African Development Bank's Independent Review Mechanism consider complaints submitted by two or more individuals.

Despite differences, IDB accountability mechanisms share certain salient traits. First, they have the competence to consider complaints submitted by individuals, groups of individuals or groups in society against an IDB. Second, the standards for assessing the conduct complained of are provided by internal rules of the IDB, that is the OP&Ps. Third, the accountability mechanism operates independently from IDB management organs and reports to IDB executive organs. IDB accountability mechanisms thereby recognize the legal relevance of the relationship between individuals and groups in society and an IDB. Such a relationship exists in many developing and economy in transition states as a result of IDB's involvement in projects in those states, including projects that implement MEAs. IDB accountability mechanisms expressly engage in executive decision-making by applying the internal rules of the IDB to specific situations. They also engage in normative development by interpreting the internal policies of the IDB in question.

Complaints to IDB accountability mechanisms typically concern several issues at the same time. The following topics frequently arise, with WBIP cases serving as examples. Lack of or deficient public participation (*India NTPC Power Generation Project*); lack of or deficient EIA (*Paraguay/Argentina Reform Project for the Water and Telecommunication Sectors (Yacyretá)*); and lack of or deficient resettlement plans or implementation of those plans (*Kenya Natural Resource Management Project*).

6.4.2   The Aarhus Convention Compliance Committee

The Aarhus Convention, in implementation of Principle 10 of the Rio Declaration (section 4.7.5), seeks to foster transparency, public participation in decision-making and access to justice in environmental matters, in its states parties and in the European Union, which is also a party to the Convention. Both the Convention and its PRTR Protocol provide for the establishment of compliance mechanisms (respectively Arts. 15 and 22). The focus in this section will be on the ACCC, given that the procedures for the functioning of the two committees are the same and that the compliance committee under the PRTR Protocol, which started its work in 2011, had in July 2015 not received any allegations concerning non-compliance.

The ACCC consists of nine members who serve in their private capacity and do not represent the state they are a national of. The ACCC may consider *submissions* from a party concerning another party's or its own compliance; *referrals* from the secretariat concerning compliance by a party and *communications* from the public regarding a party's compliance. The findings of the ACCC are not legally binding.

The ACCC had by July 2015 received two submission, no referrals and over 130 communications. Communications have been submitted by individuals and groups in society as well as NGOs and they have concerned, among other issues, the following topics. Lack of transparency due to, for example, the cost of access to documents (*ACCC/C/2008/24, Spain*); lack of or a deficient regulatory framework for public participation (*ACCC/C/2010/54, European Union*); lack of or deficient public participation because public participation was only organized after important decisions, such as the citing of a project, had already been taken (*ACCC/C/2009/41, Slovakia*); and lack of or deficient access to justice, for example because members of the public are systematically denied access to court (*ACCC/C/2008/32 Part I, European Union*) or because the costs involved in court procedures are prohibitively expensive (*ACCC/C/2008/33, United Kingdom*). In developing its findings the ACCC engages in decision-making in specific situations and by interpreting the Convention engages in normative development.

In Europe the Aarhus Convention and the findings of the ACCC have found reflection in European Union law and in the case law of the European Court of Human Rights (ECtHR). The ECtHR, like other regional human rights bodies, has read procedural human rights into substantive human rights and thereby incorporated procedural environmental rights into human rights law (section 7.2.3).

6.4.3   Procedures established by private actors

Private actors have also established accountability mechanisms to which individuals or groups in society can submit complaints. These mechanisms apply their own internal rules, often based on international and national law. Two types of mechanisms can be distinguished: accountability mechanisms established by multi-stakeholder organizations that monitor production processes for their social and environmental sustainability, such as the FSC (section 2.5), and so-called international peoples' tribunals (IPTs).

The FSC, but also the Roundtable on Sustainable Palm Oil, has established an accountability mechanism to which stakeholders can submit complaints if they find that a certified company is not acting in compliance with applicable standards. Within the FSC the mechanism is known as the FSC Dispute Resolution System. In case of a complaint the FSC, after reviewing the case, may request Accreditation Services International to conduct an investigation. Accreditation Services International is the company that manages the FSC's accreditation programme, including the quality control of FSC certification bodies. Stakeholder complaints submitted to the FSC Dispute Resolution System have resulted in findings that a certification body was in non-compliance with applicable standards and in the suspension of its right to certify for FSC (*Veracel Brazil*) as well as in certified companies having their certificate revoked (*Siforco-DRS & Danzer*). After these steps the FSC usually stays in dialogue with the body or company involved, with the object of bringing it back into compliance and thus engages in problem-solving. Problem-solving was also used the *Siforco-DRS & Danzer* case, with FSC certification being reinstated in 2014. The decisions taken by dispute resolution bodies, such as the one established by the FSC, are relevant for the development of international environmental law because they further develop applicable sustainability standards. These bodies thus participate in normative development, but, importantly, as IDB accountability mechanisms, they engage in executive decision-making.

IPTs, as national peoples' tribunals such as the Indians People's Tribunal, are usually established due to dissatisfaction with the normal court system or because there simply is no court or other body that might consider the complaint. The first example of an IPT was the Russell Tribunal established by Bertrand Russell in 1967 to examine the responsibility of the United States and its allies for the atrocities that occurred during the Vietnam War.

Examples of IPTs related to international environmental law are the 1983 International Water Tribunal, which considered pollution of the Rhine and the North Sea; the 1992 Second International Water Tribunal, which considered cases regarding water management from all over the world; the Latin American Water Tribunal, established in 1989; and the Tribunal on the International Rights of Nature, also referred to as the Tribunal on the Rights of Nature and Mother Earth, which held its first session in Ecuador in January 2014. The former two tribunals were ad hoc events held in respectively Rotterdam and Amsterdam, the Netherlands. The Latin American Water Tribunal has a permanent character with its headquarters in Costa Rica, but regularly holds sessions at various places in Latin America and has held a session in Istanbul. The Tribunal on the International Rights of Nature also has a permanent character and is associated with the Global Alliance for the Rights of Nature; it holds sessions at various places in the world. It held its second session in Lima, during the December 2014 twentieth COP of the climate change regime.

It is noteworthy that the case concerning oil exploitation by Chevron/Texaco in the Amazon region of Ecuador (section 7.5) was considered by both the Second International Water Tribunal and at the second session of the Tribunal on the International Rights of Nature. This lamentable development on the one hand may be taken to illustrate that the decisions of IPTs have no formal legal status and are extremely difficult to implement in the face of unwilling governments, private sector actors and high financial stakes. On the other hand, decisions by courts involving the same facts also do not seem to have been implemented (section 7.5).

Decisions of IPTs, at least, serve to keep the case in the public domain, illustrate deficiencies in the international and national legal systems and may infuse international environmental law with new ideas. For example, in 1983, the time of the First International Water Tribunal, it was a new idea that international environmental and human rights law be used to hold to account not only states, but also private actors. This idea has now gained broader support as illustrated by the 2011 Guiding Principles on Business and Human Rights: Implementing the United Nations "Protect, Respect and Remedy" Framework, also known as the Ruggie Principles, after John Ruggie the chairperson of the group that developed them, or as the Principles on Business and Human Rights. The Human Rights Council endorsed the Principles on Business and Human Rights in 2011 when it also established the Working Group on Business and Human Rights (Doc. A/HRC/17/L.17/Rev.1). The Principles on Business and Human Rights are based on three elements: the state duty to protect against human rights abuses by third parties, including business; the corporate responsibility to respect human rights; and greater access by victims to effective remedies, both judicial and non-judicial. The Principles also suggest that business sector actors, in addition to states, have an independent responsibility to protect and respect human rights and to provide remedies for human rights violations. To the extent that human rights incorporate international environmental law, these principles serve to hold private sector actors to account for the protection of the environment (section 7.2.2).

6.5   Assessment

Inter-state judicial dispute settlement mechanisms are rarely used in disputes involving the environment, even though when they are used they usually at least clarify and sometimes also develop the law (sections 4.5.2, 4.6.2). States similarly are reluctant to use conciliation procedures and MEA compliance mechanisms. The practice of MEA compliance mechanisms illustrates that if an independent third party plays a role in such procedures claims of non-compliance will be submitted and compliance will be reviewed. The role of the secretariats of the Montreal Protocol and CITES, as well as the expert review teams that operate within the Kyoto Protocol, illustrate this point.

Innovative developments are to be found in procedures where individuals and groups are able to access accountability mechanisms. These procedures include the accountability mechanisms established by IDBs, the ACCC and procedures such as the one established by the FSC. What makes these procedures innovative is that they create a link between what is happening on the ground and international environmental law. In creating that link these procedures recognize that the protection of the environment, as of human rights, is a concern that transcends the local, also in legal terms. The procedures established by IDBs, furthermore, recognize the legal relevance of the relationship that exists between individuals and groups in society and international actors such as the IDBs.

The ACCC, like the procedures available at IDBs and the FSC, also shows that involving individuals in non-compliance regimes entails that complaints will be received and compliance reviewed. It might be argued that in Europe, based on the Aarhus Convention and the case law of the ECtHR (section 7.2) as well as of the European Union Court of Justice, a space has developed which might be called "the Aarhus space". In this space individuals and groups in society exercise their right to protect the environment. They do so based on their, often implicit, claim before the ACCC that public authorities are hampering them in exercising this right because those authorities do not provide them with information, do not allow them to participate in decision-making or impede their right to access to justice. If this assessment is correct, "the Aarhus space" might be characterized as having eco-centric traits in that it is the protection of the environment that is the primary objective of the claims submitted, even if an individual's or group's interests may coincide with the interest of the environment.

7   The relationship with other areas of international law

7.1   Introduction

As the chapters in this book illustrate, international environmental law is a distinct area of international law in that numerous normative instruments, or parts thereof such as Part XII of the LOS Convention, can be identified that have been developed with the aim of protecting the environment. The chapters in this book also illustrate that international environmental law is inextricably linked to the body of general international law such as the law of treaties, the law on state responsibility and the law on the settlement of disputes. As such, international environmental law is part of international law. In addition, synergies or discrepancies exist between international environmental law and some other areas of international law. These other areas of international law include human rights law, the law of armed conflict, trade law and investment law. This chapter discusses the most salient synergies and discrepancies between these other areas of international law and international environmental law by focusing on how these other areas of international law engage with international environmental law.

7.2   Human rights law

The relationship between international environmental law and human rights law is reflected in the work of most United Nations human rights bodies as well as regional human rights courts and commissions. Since the 1990s, a number of special mandate holders have identified links between the enjoyment of human rights and the protection of the environment. Special mandate holders are individuals or working groups who are mandated to report on the state of affairs regarding a specific human right or a specific situation that is relevant to the protection of human rights. They are appointed by the Human Rights Council or by its predecessor, the Human Rights Commission. In 2012, the Human

Rights Council appointed John Knox as "Independent Expert on the issue of human rights obligations relating to enjoyment of a safe, clean, healthy and sustainable environment". The mandate includes identifying best practices on the use of human rights in support of environmental policy-making and making recommendations to implement the MDGs (UN doc. A/HRC/RES/19/10, 22 March 2012). In other words, the mandate holder is to identify the synergies between human rights law and international environmental law. In 2014, he presented a report that maps human rights obligations related to the environment to the Human Rights Council (Doc. A/HRC/25/53). Knox is not the only special mandate holder whose work is relevant to developing the relationship between international environmental law and human rights law. Other relevant mandates, past and present, include those related to the rights to safe drinking water and sanitation, to food and to adequate housing as well as those on hazardous substances and wastes and the situation of human right defenders.

It is generally agreed that human rights law and international environmental law are related in three main ways. First, environmental concerns have been expressed in terms of a human right to a clean or healthy environment. Second, the enjoyment of substantive human rights may be threatened by environmental degradation and conversely environmental considerations may be part of the general interest which may justify restricting protected rights. Third, procedural human rights such as the rights to the freedom of expression and association, access to information, participation in decision-making and access to justice play an important role in the realization of environmental goals.

7.2.1   The right to a clean or healthy environment

At the global level, Principle 1 of the Stockholm Declaration comes closest to formulating a human right to a clean environment. It reads as follows:

> Man has the fundamental right to freedom, equality and adequate conditions of life, in an environment of a quality that permits a life of dignity and well-being, and he bears a solemn responsibility to protect and improve the environment for present and future generations.

This formulation was not repeated in the Rio Declaration. Instead, its Principle 1 contains the following text:

Human beings are at the center of concerns for sustainable development. They are entitled to a healthy and productive life in harmony with nature.

The discrepancy between the Stockholm and Rio Declarations as well as the fact that a human right to a clean or healthy environment was not adopted at the World Summit on Sustainable Development or the Rio+20 Conference illustrate that the formulation of a human right to a clean or healthy environment remains controversial at the global level of decision-making.

At the regional level several instruments include a right to a clean or healthy environment. Article 24 of the 1981 Banjul Charter and Article 11 of the 1988 Additional Protocol to the American Convention formulate, respectively, a collective right to a "general satisfactory environment favorable to their development" and an individual right "to live in a healthy environment". Other regional human rights instruments such as the 2004 Arab Charter of Human Rights and the 2012 Association of Southeast Asian Nations (ASEAN) Human Rights Declaration formulate a right to a healthy or clean environment as part of the right to an adequate standard of living. In Europe, Article 1 of the Aarhus Convention provides "the right of every person of present and future generations to live in an environment adequate to his or her health and well-being". An increasing number of national constitutions also formulate a right to a clean environment, using various terms.

7.2.2   Substantive human rights

Environmental problems such as climate change, loss of biological diversity, improper handling of hazardous wastes or resource exploitation can threaten the enjoyment of human rights. Think of the consequences of climate change, such as flooding of low-lying coastal areas, the disappearance of small island states and increased desertification. These developments threaten the lives of many, often lead to displacement and involve a host of human rights, including, in the case of small island states, the right to self-determination. Also think of local populations, including indigenous peoples, who may see their right to food impaired and their livelihood destroyed as a result of the disappearance of tropical rainforest. Finally, consider the contamination of soil and air due to illegal dumping of hazardous wastes or the unregulated exploitation of oil, which may threaten, among other rights, the rights to life, private and family life, health, food and water.

The above are only a few examples of how substantive human rights may be threatened by environmental degradation. Some global human rights treaties recognize this link. For example, Article 24 of the 1989 Convention on the Rights of the Child, requires that the "risks of environmental pollution" are to be taken "into consideration" in the implementation of "the right of the child to the enjoyment of the highest attainable standard of health". In a similar vein, Article 12 of the 1966 International Covenant on Economic, Social and Cultural Rights (ICESCR) provides that to achieve the right to the highest attainable standard of physical and mental health "all aspects of environmental and industrial hygiene" shall be improved. The Committee on Economic, Social and Cultural Rights has linked this provision to, among other rights, the right to water and sanitation. Moreover, the 1989 ILO Convention 169, on indigenous and tribal peoples, recognizes the special cultural and spiritual relationship that indigenous peoples have with their lands and environment and requires that these be protected (Part II). The relationship between indigenous peoples, their culture, their lands and the environment is also recognized in other human rights instruments and in the Biodiversity Convention and its Nagoya Protocol (section 4.5.6).

Regional human rights bodies, such as the African Commission on Human and People's Rights (ACHPR), the ECtHR and the Inter-American Commission on Human Rights and Inter-American Court of Human Rights (resp. IAComHR and IACtHR) have all ruled that human rights can be violated as a result of environmental degradation. Relevant rights include the right to life, the right to health, the right to property and the right to family and private life. Landmark rulings include those of the ACHPR in the *Ogoniland Case*; the ECtHR in *López Ostra v. Spain*, *Öneryildiz v. Turkey*, *Taşkin and others v. Turkey* and *Fadeyeva v. Russia*; the IAComHR in *Maya Indigenous Community of the Toledo District v. Belize*; and the IACtHR in *Saramaka People v. Suriname* and in *Kichwa Indigenous People of Sarayaku v. Ecuador*. Conversely, courts and tribunals have also ruled that, if properly balanced, environmental law, as part of the general interest, may provide a justification for limiting human rights – the ruling of the ECtHR in *Hatton v. UK* provides an example.

The above-mentioned rulings illustrate that states have a duty to have in place proper legal and enforcement systems for realizing the human rights in question, including relevant environmental aspects. Beyond that, and importantly, the rulings also show that states have the positive duty to ensure that private sector actors do not infringe these same human rights while engaging in their activities. Human rights bodies, however, have not established an independent responsibility for private sector actors, as suggested by the Principles on Business and Human Rights (section 6.4.3). This is because human rights are generally regarded as only applying vertically, that is between a state and individuals and groups in society, and not horizontally, that is between individuals and groups in society, even if states have a positive duty to ensure that human rights are not violated in such horizontal relationships.

7.2.3   Procedural human rights

Principle 10 of the Rio Declaration highlights the importance of procedural environmental rights, rights which, as discussed in section 4.7.5, have found their way into international environmental law in various ways, including the Aarhus Convention discussed in section 6.4.2.

Two aspects are briefly touched upon in this section. First, the importance of the right to freedom of expression, which includes the freedom to seek, receive and impart information, and the freedom of association for environmental human rights defenders, including both individuals and groups, such as NGOs. These individuals and groups regularly face threats, intimidation, attacks and killings from state and non-state actors, as the work of the Special Rapporteur on the situation of human rights defenders illustrates.

Second, human rights courts and tribunals have not only recognized that environmental degradation can result in violations of human rights. They have also recognized that in order to prevent such violations procedural rights such as the right to environmental information (including the duty to collect environmental information), the right to participation in decision-making and the right to access to justice are crucial. Significantly, human rights courts and commissions have read these rights into the substantive human rights at stake. The rulings mentioned in the previous section illustrate this development. For example, in the *Ogoniland Case*, *Taşkin* and *Kichwa Indigenous People of Sarayaku v. Ecuador* procedural rights were read into, respectively, the rights to health and to a satisfactory environment, the right to family and private life and the property rights of an indigenous people (section 7.2.2). Procedural rights have thereby become part of the substantive human rights protected by the instruments in question.

7.3   The law of armed conflict

Armed conflict clearly can result in significant damage to the environment. Think of, for example, the use of defoliants, such as Agent Orange, by the United States in the Vietnam War during the 1960s and early 1970s; the burning of Kuwait's oilfields by the Iraqi army in 1991, at the end of the First Gulf War; the effects of the use of landmines on the use of land for agricultural and other purposes; and the contamination of water. Principles 24 and 25 of the Rio Declaration expressly link environmental concerns to armed conflict. The first sentence of Principle 24 provides that "[w]arfare is inherently destructive of sustainable development" and Principle 25 provides that "[p]eace, development and environmental protection are interdependent and indivisible".

Two main themes arise in the relationship between international environmental law and the law of armed conflict, also known as the law of warfare and international humanitarian law. First, the extent to which the law of armed conflict, that is, the 1977 Additional Protocol I to the 1949 Geneva Conventions (Additional Protocol I) and treaties prohibiting the use of certain means or methods of armed conflict and disarmament treaties, limits the means of engaging in armed conflict and thereby serves to protect the environment. Second, the extent to which international environmental law applies in situations of armed conflict. These two themes have been the subject of studies published by the International Committee of the Red Cross, are currently on the agenda of the ILC and will be discussed below.

7.3.1   The law of armed conflict and the protection of the environment

Environmental considerations may be part of the law of armed conflict by way of two paths: by way of the so-called Martens Clause, in Article 1(2) of Additional Protocol I, and by way of prohibitions to use certain means of warfare contained in Additional Protocol I or in specific treaties. Such prohibitions in most cases indirectly serve to protect the environment, their main aim being to protect civilians and related interests.

The Martens Clause reads as follows:

> In cases not covered by this Protocol or by other international agreements, civilians and combatants remain under the protection and authority of the

principles of international law derived from established custom, from the principles of humanity and from the dictates of public conscience.

Certain principles of international environmental law might well be regarded as deriving from established custom, principles of humanity and the dictates of public conscience. One might consider the implications of, for example, the prevention, precautionary and integration principles as well as principles regarding the common concern of humankind and inter- and intra-generational equity for the conduct of armed conflict.

Additional Protocol I provides that the means of waging armed conflict are not unlimited (Art. 35(1)) and prohibits certain means and methods of engaging in armed conflict. Two articles specifically refer to the environment. Article 35(3) prohibits the use of "methods or means of warfare which are intended, or may be expected, to cause widespread, long-term and severe damage to the natural environment" and Article 55(2) prohibits "[a]ttacks against the natural environment by way of reprisals". Article 55(1) furthermore provides that:

> Care shall be taken in warfare to protect the natural environment against widespread, long-term and severe damage. This protection includes a prohibition of the use of methods or means of warfare which are intended or may be expected to cause such damage to the natural environment and thereby to prejudice the health or survival of the population.

Other provisions in Additional Protocol I that prohibit specific types of attacks and may serve to protect the environment, even if their main aim is to protect civilians and related interests, include: the general prohibition to use methods of warfare "of a nature to cause superfluous injury or unnecessary suffering" (Art. 35(2)) and the prohibition to attack "installations containing dangerous forces, namely dams, dykes and nuclear electrical generating stations" (Art. 56(1)). The latter provision, however, is subject to the exception that the attack may proceed if it is the only feasible way of securing that the use of these installations "in regular, significant and direct support of military operations" is terminated (Art. 56(2)(a) and (b)), thereby taking away from its potential to protect the environment. Additional Protocol I also determines that such attacks are war crimes if they are undertaken "in the knowledge that such attack will cause excessive loss of life, injury to civilians or damage to civilian objects" (Art. 85(3) (c)). Here, as in Article 35(3), we see the high threshold for prohibited activities that is characteristic of the law on armed conflict. It requires "intent/expectation" or, in case of Article 85(3)(c), "knowledge" and "widespread, long-term and severe" damage to the environment or "excessive loss" to civilian interests.

The 1977 Convention on the Prohibition of Military or Any Hostile Use of Environmental Modification Techniques (ENMOD Convention), as Additional Protocol I, expressly prohibits certain acts aimed at damaging the environment during armed conflict. Its parties undertake not to engage in "military or any other hostile use of environmental modification techniques having widespread, long-lasting or severe effects as the means of destruction, damage or injury to any other State Party" (Art. 1(1)). "Environmental modification techniques" are defined as "any technique for changing – through the deliberate manipulation of natural processes – the dynamics, composition or structure of the Earth, including its biota, lithosphere, hydrosphere and atmosphere, or of outer space" (Art. 2). As in Additional Protocol I, the threshold for prohibited activities is a high one, involving both "deliberate manipulation" and "widespread, long-lasting and severe effects". In addition to the ENMOD Convention, the 1980 Convention on Certain Conventional Weapons in its preamble recalls the prohibition to use means of warfare "which are intended or may be expected, to cause widespread, long-term and severe damage to the environment". Moreover, the 1998 Statute of the International Criminal Court (ICC Statute) is relevant in this context. Its Article 8(2)(b)(iv), provides that the following constitutes a war crime:

> Intentionally launching an attack in the knowledge that such attack will cause incidental loss of life or injury to civilians or damage to civilian objects or widespread, long-term and severe damage to the natural environment which would be clearly excessive in relation to the concrete and direct overall military advantage anticipated . . .

The ICC Statute thus, as the instruments discussed above, also provides a high threshold for prohibited activities. In this case "intent" and "knowledge" as well as "widespread, long-term and severe" damage to the environment are required. In addition, a consideration of proportionality between the environmental damage and the military aim – "clearly excessive in relation to" – applies.

Other treaties that may serve the protection of the environment in times of armed conflict, even if this is not their primary focus, include those on the means of engaging in armed conflict or on disarmament. Relevant examples are: the 1954 Hague Convention for the Protection of Cultural Property, the 1968 Non-Proliferation Treaty, the 1972 Biological Weapons Convention, the 1997 Anti-Personnel Mines Convention and the 2008 Convention on Cluster Munitions.

7.3.2   International environmental law in times of armed conflict

There is considerable uncertainty, and debate, whether and if so to what extent international environmental law applies during armed conflict; this is due to the content of both the law of armed conflict and of international environmental law. Principle 24 of the Rio Declaration reflects this uncertainty when, after the sentence cited above (section 7.3), it reads as follows:

> States shall therefore respect international law providing protection for the environment in times of armed conflict and cooperate in its further development, as necessary.

This provision leaves it undecided whether states should apply international environmental law, also during armed conflict, or whether they should apply the law of armed conflict to the extent that it seeks to protect the environment. The ICJ did not clarify this uncertainty in *Nuclear Weapons*. Instead it held that together, Principle 24 of the Rio Declaration and the provisions of Additional Protocol I related to the environment, namely Articles 34(3) and 55 (section 7.3.1):

> embody a general obligation to protect the natural environment against widespread, long-term and severe environmental damage; the prohibition of methods and means of warfare which are intended, or may be expected, to cause such damage; and the prohibition of attacks against the natural environment by way of reprisals. (para. 31)

The threshold for prohibited activities set by the Court clearly is the same one we encounter in the law of armed conflict: there must be "intent" or "expectation" that "widespread, long-term and severe damage" to the environment will ensue as a result of the activities engaged in. Such an approach does not reflect the prevention principle let alone the precautionary principle, which determine when action to protect the environment is to be taken under international environmental law (section 4.6). The ICJ in this case also held that even if international environmental law did not expressly prohibit the use of nuclear weapons, it "indicates important environmental factors that are properly to be taken into account in the context of the implementation of the principles and rules of the law applicable in armed conflict" (para. 33). The ICJ thereby characterizes international environmental law as providing factors that are to be taken into account, but not as a body of law that provides duties that states are to comply with. The ICJ, moreover, by holding that it could not "reach a definitive conclusion on the legality or illegality of nuclear weapons by a State in an extreme circumstance of self-defence, in which its very survival would be at stake" (para. 97), indicated that the principle of proportionality, which is an important element of the law of armed conflict, also applies, even if under strict conditions – the very survival of the state – when considering the use of nuclear weapons. The ICJs' approach in *Nuclear Weapons* clearly resounds with the system of the law on armed conflict. It might be queried what is being protected here: might it be the state as the essential building block of international law as we know it?

The ILC's Special Rapporteur on the protection of the environment in relation to armed conflict, Marie Jacobsson, has suggested that approaching the protection of the environment in armed conflict mainly through "the lens of the laws of warfare, including international humanitarian law" constitutes too narrow a perspective "as modern international law recognises that the international law applicable during armed conflict may be wider than the laws of warfare" (UNDOC A/66/10, Annex E, para. 2). The ILC placed the topic "protection of the environment in relation to armed conflict" on its long-term programme of work in 2011 and considered a preliminary report on the topic in 2014 (UNDOC A/CN.4/674 and Corr.1). The report, among other things, presents an overview of relevant international environmental law principles and concepts as well as an examination of the relationship between international environmental and human rights law. The latter suggests that human rights law, to the extent that it incorporates international environmental law (section 7.2), may be relevant for incorporating environmental considerations into the law of armed conflict.

Uncertainty as to whether international environmental law applies during armed conflict also arises because most international environmental instruments do not provide an unequivocal answer to the question whether they apply during armed conflict; instead they remain silent on the matter. There are a few exceptions to this rule. The 1959 Antarctic Treaty provides that Antarctica shall be used for peaceful purposes only and prohibits "any measures of a military nature" (Art. 1). The LOS Convention determines that the Area shall be used "exclusively for peaceful purposes" (Art. 141). The Watercourses Convention provides that watercourses and related installations shall be protected according to the rules of armed conflict (Art. 29). It thereby incorporates Article 56(1) of Additional Protocol I to the Geneva Conventions, to the extent that this later provision refers to dams and dykes, and it expands on this provision by also referring to watercourses themselves and related installations in general. Treaties related to civil liability for environmental damage as a rule exclude liability for damage originating in armed conflict.

7.4   Trade law

Principle 12 of the Rio Declaration illustrates the dilemmas involved in reconciling international environmental and international trade law. It reads as follows:

> States should cooperate to promote a supportive and open international economic system that would lead to economic growth and sustainable development in all countries, to better address the problems of environmental degradation. Trade policy measures for environmental purposes should not constitute a means of arbitrary or unjustifiable discrimination or a disguised restriction on international trade.
>
> Unilateral actions to deal with environmental challenges outside the jurisdiction of the importing country should be avoided. Environmental measures addressing transboundary or global environmental problems should, as far as possible, be based on an international consensus.

This provision on the one hand regards free trade as a means to achieve sustainable development and protection of the environment. On the other hand, it provides that trade-related environmental measures are subject to the disciplines of international trade law. Moreover, it suggests that international consensus, as opposed to unilateral measures, is the preferred way of addressing transboundary or global environmental problems. It is precisely these dilemmas that have arisen in cases before the dispute settlement forums of the WTO.

The prominent role played by the WTO dispute settlement forums, panels and in particular the Appellate Body, is due to several factors. First, the WTO law, as opposed to international environmental law, provides a system for compulsory binding dispute settlement, which means that parties to the WTO have consented to the WTO dispute settlement bodies exercising jurisdiction over their disputes (section 6.1). Second, WTO member states disagree as to how environmental considerations should be incorporated into WTO law, as evidenced by the lack of progress achieved by the Committee on Trade and Environment and the difficult ongoing negotiations on the topic in the Doha Round. Third, sustainable development and the protection of the environment are part of the aims of the WTO. The first paragraph of the preamble of the 1994 Agreement Establishing the World Trade Organization (WTO Agreement) provides that free trade is to be realized while

> allowing for the optimal use of the world's resources in accordance with the objective of sustainable development, seeking both to protect and preserve the environment and to enhance the means for doing so in a manner consistent with their respective needs and concerns at different levels of economic development.

In specific WTO agreements, such as the General Agreement on Tariffs and Trade (GATT), the SPS Agreement, the Agreement on Technical Barriers to Trade (TBT Agreement) and the Agreement on Subsidies and Countervailing Measures (SCM Agreement), all concluded in 1994, concerns regarding the environment generally manifest themselves as exceptions to rules regarding free trade. GATT Article XX(b) and (g) allows states to take measures "necessary for the protection of human, animal or plant life" and to ensure "the conservation of exhaustible natural resources"; the SPS Agreement allows states to take measures "necessary for the protection of human, animal or plant life or health" (Art. 2(1)) and the TBT Agreement provides that a TBT measure may be adopted to ensure the "protection of human health or safety, animal or plant life or health, or the environment" (Art. 2(2)). Such measures must meet conditions related to necessity, proportionality and non-discrimination and must be adequately reasoned based on scientific principles and risk assessment (section 4.7.4). The SCM Agreement, prohibits some subsidies (export and local content requirements, Art. 3) but allows others provided they meet certain conditions (Arts. 5–6) (section 7.4.5). Moreover, under the SPS and TBT Agreements international standards are leading in determining whether a measure is in conformity with these agreements.

WTO law and international environmental law thus may meet because MEAs, as discussed above (sections 2.2.1, 3.4.2, 3.4.3, 3.5), use trade measures to protect the environment. In addition, states use a variety of unilateral trade-related measures to protect the environment. Examples of such measures include: import restrictions on the import of certain goods with the aim of protecting the environment within the jurisdiction of a state or extra-territorially; export restrictions with the aim of preserving natural resources or protecting nature within the jurisdiction of a state; product standards regarding, for example, labelling or recycling; and subsidies to stimulate environmentally friendly means of production within the jurisdiction of a state.

The rest of this section illustrates how the WTO dispute settlement forums have dealt with the most prominent junctures at which WTO law and international environmental law may meet. These include MEA-based trade measures; unilateral import restrictions under the GATT; the SPS Agreement and the precautionary principle; the TBT Agreement and labelling requirements; and the SCM Agreement and environmental subsidies This section is by no means exhaustive, it does not deal with all the junctures at which WTO law and environmental law meet nor does it treat the chosen topics comprehensively.

7.4.1   MEAs-based trade measures

As discussed elsewhere in this book, MEAs use a variety of trade measures for the protection of the environment. The measures include CITES prohibiting or regulating trade in endangered species of fauna and flora (section 2.2); the Montreal Protocol prohibiting the use of and trade in ozone-depleting substances (section 3.4.2); the Kyoto Protocol creating a market in emission reduction units for its parties (section 3.4.3); and a large number of MEAs employing prior informed consent regimes to regulate trade in hazardous substances (section 3.5.1). While commentators have regularly speculated on the compatibility of these trade measures with WTO law, to date these measures have not been challenged before the dispute settlement forums of the WTO.

The Appellate Body, however, had the opportunity to express itself on the role of MEAs in the 1998 *US–Shrimp* case. The case concerned the unilateral introduction by the United States of measures prohibiting the import of shrimp caught without so-called turtle excluder devices in place with the aim of protecting species of sea turtles listed on CITES Appendix I. The Appellate Body criticized the fact that the United States had not entered into serious negotiations with the complainant states with the objective of concluding bilateral or multilateral agreements for purposes of protecting sea turtles and encouraged the United States to engage in such negotiations (para.166 and following). The Appellate Body thereby suggested that it might well uphold internationally agreed environmental measures.

7.4.2   The GATT and unilateral import restrictions

In assessing whether unilateral trade measures that seek to protect the environment are compatible with GATT rules the Appellate Body uses a two-tiered approach. It first ascertains whether the measures at stake come within the ambit of the exceptions contained in Article XX (b) and (g). If it finds this to be the case, it then considers whether the measures meet the conditions of the chapeaux of Article XX.

The chapeau of Article XX and its paragraphs (b) and (g) provide as follows:

> Subject to the requirement that such measures are not applied in a manner which would constitute a means of arbitrary or unjustifiable discrimination between countries where the same conditions prevail, or a disguised restriction on international trade, nothing in this Agreement shall be construed to prevent the adoption or enforcement by any contracting party of measures:
>
> . . .
>
> (b) necessary to protect human, animal or plant life or health;
>
> . . .
>
> (g) relating to the conservation of exhaustible natural resources if such measures are made effective in conjunction with restrictions on domestic production or consumption . . .

In deciding whether a measure meets the conditions of paragraph (b) or (g) of Article XX the Appellate Body has ruled on what constitutes the protection of "human, animal or plant life or health" and interpreted the term "necessary" in paragraph (b) and the terms "natural resources", "relating to" and "made effective in conjunction with restrictions on domestic production or consumption" in paragraph (g).

In respect of Article XX(b), panels and the Appellate Body have considered a wide range of environmental, and health, measures to come within the ambit of the terms "human, animal and plant life or health". They have in the course of this process developed the meaning of term "necessary" in the case law over a significant period of time. The leading case currently is the Appellate Body's 2007 decision in *Brazil–Retreaded Tyres*. In this case the Appellate Body held that in determining whether a measure is necessary consideration must be given to in particular "the importance of the interests or values at stake, the extent of the contribution to the achievement of the measures objective, and its trade restrictiveness" and the measure must be compared to alternatives in terms of trade restrictiveness and the objectives at stake (para. 178). It thereby introduced something akin to a proportionality test. In 2001, the Appellate Body in *EC–Asbestos* also determined that it is for the member state concerned to determine the level of protection it considers appropriate. In other words, the level of protection cannot be challenged by other member states, only the necessity of the measure in achieving the level of protection (para. 168). The Appellate Body also ruled on the burden of proof in such cases. It determined that it is for the state that has adopted the measure to show that the measure is necessary and for the state challenging the measure to identify possible alternative measures (*Brazil–Retreaded Tyres*, para. 156). In showing necessity in the face of scientific uncertainty the Appellate Body further held that a state in discharging its burden of proof may "rely in good faith, on scientific sources, which at the time, may represent a divergent, but qualified and respected, opinion" and need not "automatically follow, what at a given time, may constitute a majority scientific opinion" (para. 178).

The Appellate Body's decision in *US–Shrimp* is still currently the leading case on the interpretation of Article XX(g). The Appellate Body has adopted an evolutionary approach to the interpretation of the term "natural resources" by providing that the term must be interpreted "in the light of contemporary concerns of the community of nations about the protection of the environment" (paras. 129–30). It furthermore held that a resource may be living or non-living and that it need not be rare or endangered in order to qualify as exhaustible (para. 131). A second question that has arisen with respect to Article XX(g) relates to the meaning of the term "relating to". In *US–Shrimp* the

Appellate Body held that the measures must be "reasonably related to the ends" they seek to protect, in this case sea turtles (para. 141). The phrase "made effective in conjunction with restrictions on domestic production or consumption" was interpreted by the Appellate Body in its 1996 decision in *US–Gasoline*. It held that domestic production or consumption of the same product should be subject to comparable "even-handed" restrictions, implying that the restrictions need not be identical (paras. 20–1; also see *US–Shrimp*, para. 144). Lastly, the Appellate Body in *US–Shrimp* clarified that Article XX(g) also applies to the conservation of exhaustible resources in areas beyond national jurisdiction (paras. 132–3).

As a result of the above-mentioned interpretations, a larger number of environmental measures as well as those related to health are now likely to come within the scope of the exceptions contained in Article XX(b) or (g). However, as mentioned above, there is a second tier to the test: applying the chapeau. The chapeau determines that measures may not constitute "arbitrary discrimination", "unjustifiable discrimination" or "a disguised restriction on international trade". In *US–Shrimp* the Appellate Body determined that "the paragraphs of Article XX set forth *limited and conditional* exceptions from the obligations of the substantive provisions" (emphasis in original, para. 157); that the chapeau is "one expression of the principle of good faith" which seeks to avoid the abuse of rights and to ensure that rights are used reasonably (para. 158). The task of interpreting and applying the chapeau in a given case according to the Appellate Body then is "one of locating and marking out a line of equilibrium between the right of a Member to invoke an exception under Article XX and the rights of the other Members under varying substantive provisions" (para. 159). With the Appellate Body emphasizing that the line of equilibrium is not static (para. 159) and that the standards set by the chapeau involve "both substantive and procedural requirements" (para. 160). It is within this context that the measures in question in *US–Shrimp* were found to constitute both arbitrary discrimination and unjustifiable discrimination. They were found to constitute arbitrary discrimination because the United States rigidly recognized only one way of protecting turtles when catching shrimp and did not consider the situation in other states (para. 182); they were found to constitute unjustifiable discrimination because the United States did not engage in serious negotiations with the states concerned, even if it had negotiated with other states (para. 171).

7.4.3   The SPS Agreement and the precautionary principle

This section is devoted to unilateral measures under the SPS Agreement because relevant case law provides an illustration of how the Appellate Body has dealt with scientific uncertainty and the precautionary principle in the context of the protection of health (section 4.6.2). SPS measures may concern, for example, food safety or the protection against pests or diseases. They may be adopted when "necessary for the protection of human, animal or plant life or health" (Art. 2(1)) and thus could include environmental measures.

Article 3(3) of the SPS Agreement provides exceptions to the general rule of the SPS Agreement, namely that international standards, guidelines or recommendations determine the level of protection that a state may require. It allows WTO member states to introduce a higher level of protection if there is scientific justification or based on an assessment of risk which meets the conditions set out in Article 5 of the SPS Agreement. Thus, contrary to exceptions under GATT Article XX(b) (section 7.4.2) a state may not unconditionally determine the appropriate level of protection under the SPS Agreement. Furthermore, in case of insufficient scientific evidence, a state may adopt provisional SPS measures on the basis of available and relevant information and must review the measures within a reasonable time, based on available information (Art. 5(7)).

With regards to the relationship between the precautionary principle and the SPA Agreement, the Appellate Body in *EC–Hormones* acknowledged that the SPS Agreement in paragraph 6 of its preamble, in Article 3(3) and in Article 5(7) reflects the precautionary principle (para. 124). However, in the same case, the Appellate Body also limited the application of the precautionary principle to Article 5(7) and determined that, even if it were a principle of customary international law, it could not override Article 5(1) and (2) of the SPS Agreement, setting out standards for conducting risk assessments (paras. 123–5).

With respect to scientific uncertainty and the risk assessment on which a member state may base a higher level of protection, the Appellate Body pointed out that scientific controversy does not prevent risk assessments from being undertaken and that Article 5(1) of the SPS Agreement allows states to base SPS measures on divergent or minority views provided the source is qualified or respected (para. 591, *US–Continued Suspension*). In the same case the Appellate Body also held that the risk assessment upon which the higher level of protection is based need not consider the same parameters and conduct the same research as the risk assessment underlying the relevant international standard (para. 534). The Appellate Body thereby created some room for divergent views on appropriate levels of protection in view of scientific uncertainty.

The Appellate Body in several cases has found that the reference to scientific uncertainty in Article 5(7) means that it reflects the precautionary principle. However, in *Japan–Measures Affecting the Importation of Apples* the Appellate Body limited the role of the precautionary principle in the context of Article 5(7) by distinguishing insufficient scientific evidence from scientific uncertainty (para. 184) and determining that scientific uncertainty – difference of opinion among scientists – does not trigger the option of adopting provisional SPS measures. However, in determining the meaning of the term "insufficient" in Article 5(7) in *US–Continued Suspension* the Appellate Body found the following:

> The "insufficiency" requirement in Article 5.7 does not imply that new scientific evidence must entirely displace the scientific evidence upon which an international standard relies. It suffices that new scientific developments call into question whether the body of scientific evidence still permits of a sufficiently objective assessment of risk. (para. 725)

The Appellate Body thus also in this case created some room for divergent views on what might be appropriate provisional SPS measures in view of scientific uncertainty.

7.4.4   The TBT Agreement and environmental labelling schemes

Environmental considerations have arisen under the TBT Agreement in relation to the labelling schemes for environmentally friendly produced goods. The leading case at present is *US–Tuna II*. At issue in the dispute was the United States scheme to label tuna caught in a dolphin-friendly way and in particular the denial of the label to tuna products from Mexico. The Appellate Body determined that the labelling scheme in question was indeed a technical regulation within the meaning of the TBT Agreement (para. 199). It also found the denial of the label to Mexican tuna products modified market conditions to the detriment of Mexican tuna (para. 240). However, it found the labelling scheme not to be even-handed because it only considered the detrimental effects for dolphins of certain fishing methods for tuna and not other fishing methods. As a result it found the scheme to be inconsistent with Article 2(1) of the TBT Agreement because Mexican tuna products were treated less favourably than those originating in the United States or other states (para. 299).

In the same case the Appellate Body also provided insight into the characteristics that an international standard-setting body must meet under the TBT Agreement. Such bodies are important under the TBT Agreement because international standards, based on Article 2(4) of the TBT Agreement, are to form the basis for technical regulations adopted by member states. Based on various definitions of international standards and standard-setting bodies, in particular those of the International Organization for Standardization (ISO), the Appellate Body found that the 1998 Agreement on the International Dolphin Conservation Programme (AIDCP) is not an international standardizing body for purposes of the TBT Agreement (para. 399). It came to this finding because the AIDCP "is not open to the relevant bodies of at least all Members" (para. 399). Instead, membership of AIDCP is by invitation. As a result of the Appellate Bodies finding a "dolphin-safe definition and certification" adopted by the AIDCP did not qualify as an international standard (para. 399).

The ruling in *US–Tuna II* raises the question how WTO relates to private standard-setting entities such as the FSC, a question that has attracted a significant amount of attention in relation to the SPS Agreement.

7.4.5   The SCM Agreement and environmental subsidies

In recent years, cases involving subsidies for the production of renewable energy have been submitted to the WTO. One of these, *Canada–Renewable Energy*, has been decided by the Appellate Body; two other cases have been the subject of consultations for extended periods of time.[1]

In *Canada–Renewable Energy*, the Appellate Body had to decide whether a feed-in-tariff (FIT), a guaranteed price for electricity

---

1 *European Union and Certain Member States – Certain Measures Affecting the Renewable Energy Generation Sector*, the request for consultation was submitted by China in November 2012. *India – Certain Measures Relating to Solar Cells and Solar Modules*, the request for consultation was submitted by the United States in February 2013.

generated, which was conditional on the generator meeting local content requirements, constituted a prohibited subsidy under the WTO law, including the SCM Agreement. It found that the local content requirement as such was contrary to WTO law, the GATT and the 1994 Agreement on Trade-Related Investment Measures (TRIMs Agreement) in particular (para. 5.85).

The decision also addressed the question what should be the relevant benchmark market for determining whether the subsidy constituted a benefit, the energy market in general or the market for renewable energy. The Appellate Body concluded that the relevant market is the renewable energy market and that government interference in such a market does not constitute a prohibited subsidy in terms of the SCM Agreement, based on the argument that this market would not exist without a government interfering (paras. 5.188–5.191).

The decision has been criticized on mainly two accounts. First, it has been argued that FITs are not viable without local content requirements and that these should thus be allowed in order to stimulate the generation of renewable energy. Second, it has been submitted that the energy market in general should be the benchmark and that government subsidies to renewable energy production should be allowed on that market because the environmental consequences of the emission of GHGs are not generally internalized in electricity prices on that market.

7.5 Investment law

International investment law was developed to protect foreign direct investment from measures by host states that diminish the value of the investment, such as expropriations and other treatment deemed to be unfair. International investment law consists of a series of regional treaties, such as the 1992 North American Free Trade Agreement (NAFTA), and thousands of bilateral investment treaties (BITs). While the substantive provisions of investment treaties vary, most contain provisions on equitable and fair treatment and on the right to compensation in case of expropriation. In addition, most investment treaties provide that both host-home state disputes and investor-state disputes are to be settled by international arbitration and, in the case of investor-state disputes, generally do not require that the investor exhaust local remedies.

The manner in which environmental concerns, and public concerns more in general, have been considered in investor-state arbitrations has raised concern. This has been the case in particular because arbitral tribunals have either ignored environment concerns (*Metalclad v. Mexico*) or have held that even if the pursuit of environmental protection is a laudable public purpose, it does not affect the obligation to compensate (*Santa Elena v. Costa Rica* and *Tecmed v. Mexico*). The *Santa Elena* case concerned expropriation by Costa Rica for environmental reasons; in the *Tecmed* case environmental measures were at stake and the manner in which they were applied was found to amount to expropriation. The decisions in these cases have given rise to the question whether they might have a "chilling" effect on the adoption of environmental law and regulations. These concerns have also been raised in Australia and Europe in relation to the Trans-Pacific Partnership Agreement and the Trans-Atlantic Trade Investment Partnership. However, arbitral decisions holding that environmental concerns indeed involve public purposes and do not involve expropriation, and thus do not give rise to compensation, have also been delivered (*Methanex v. US*), as have arbitral decisions in which environmental concerns are addressed but where the claim failed on other grounds such as lacking fairness or failing to meet the least-restrictive-measure test (*S.D. Meyer v. Canada*).

While the case law mentioned above might suggest that it remains to be seen how investor-state arbitrations may evolve in considering environmental concerns, a bigger issue may be involved in investor-state arbitrations: the disempowering of local courts and as a result local populations.

Consider the following situation. Various national courts in Ecuador, the host state, in courts in Argentina, Canada, Brazil and the United States and before three BIT-based arbitral tribunals at the PCA have considered or are considering cases concerning oil exploitation in the Ecuadorian Amazon involving Chevron/Texaco, successor companies that operated in Ecuador up until the early 1990s. These cases are referred to as the Chevron/Texaco or Lago Agrio cases, after the region concerned. Note that these cases involve one of the situations that was considered by the Second International Water Tribunal in 1992 (section 6.4.3) and concern facts similar to those considered in *Kichwa Indigenous People of Sarayaku v. Ecuador* in 2012 by the IACtHR (section 7.2.2) and by the Tribunal on the International Rights of Nature in December 2014 (section 6.4.3). While it is beyond the scope of this book to comment on all the various past and pending cases, it is worthy of note that the local population reportedly continues to live in a seriously degraded environment.

How might the investor-state arbitrations that are part of the Lago Agrio cases be regarded? First, while investor-state arbitrations, like the accountability procedures discussed in section 6.4, may be taken to convey that investments matter beyond the local. However, as opposed to the procedures discussed in section 6.4, the local seems very far removed from these arbitrations. Second, due to the absence of an obligation to exhaust local remedies for investors, these investor-state disputes are taken out of their local context. This entails that members of the local population, who are most likely to experience the results of the environmental degradation involved, are not a party to or cannot otherwise participate in these proceedings. Investor-state arbitrations, contrary to IDB-based grievance mechanisms (section 6.4.1) and the procedure available at the FSC (section 6.4.3), then, would seem to deny the legal relevance of the relationship between individuals and groups in society and a multilateral private sector actor that operates in that society. This is one of the concerns that also seems to inform some of the questions that are being posed regarding the Trans-Pacific Partnership Agreement and the Trans-Atlantic Trade Investment Partnership: the disempowerment of local courts and local populations.

A requirement to exhaust local remedies in those cases where public interests are involved in investor-state disputes would serve to retain the link between the local and global contexts, both of which are involved in these cases. Think of a national court that knows that its judgment might be scrutinized by an international court or tribunal and an international court or tribunal that will have to evaluate various national judgments originating in different jurisdictions.

7.6   Assessment

One might capture the relationship between international environmental law and the other areas of law discussed as follows. Clear synergies exist between human rights law and international environmental law. It is particularly remarkable how regional human rights bodies have integrated procedural environmental rights into substantive human rights. The relationship between the law on armed conflict and international environmental law remains fraught with uncertainties and its systemic development has only recently been taken up by the ILC. The relationship between international trade law and international environmental law is contentious, with WTO member states not being able to agree on how to integrate the two areas of law. As a result the Appellate Body has had to take on, and increasingly is taking on, the challenge of finding synergies between the two bodies of law. The relationship between investment law and international environmental law is particularly contentious, especially because the arbitration system that is part of investment law disengages the local and the global.

Two additional points arise from the analysis conducted in this chapter. First, systematic consideration of the relationship between international environmental law and other areas of law, beyond dispute settlement procedures, seems to be taking place at two sites within the United Nations. For the relationship between human rights law and international environmental law this site is formed by United Nations human rights treaty bodies and especially the United Nations special mandate holders. For the relationship between the law of armed conflict and international environmental law the site is the ILC. At these two sites the integration principle (section 4.7.1) is being implemented. Second, the relationship between international environmental law and other areas of international law is defined by courts and tribunals available in other areas of international law: by human rights courts, the WTO Appellate Body and arbitral tribunals in investor-state arbitrations. Together these two points suggest that international environmental law is not in the lead when it comes to defining its relationship to other bodies of international law, even if UNEP under its Montevideo IV Programme is currently also focusing on the relationship between international environmental law and other areas of law (section 2.5).

8 Conclusion: continuity and change

8.1 Introduction

Having traced the development of international environmental law from its early beginnings in the late nineteenth/early twentieth centuries, this book returns to one of its earlier themes: continuity and change (section 2.2). This chapter adopts a bird's-eye perspective in taking stock of just over a century of international legal developments as related to the environment. It identifies salient continuities and changes in international environmental law and in doing so also marks some of the challenges that this body of law faces. This chapter considers the following themes: the relationship between developed and developing states; institutional fragmentation; emerging similarities between the roles of NGOs and private sector actors; linking the local and the global in regulatory approaches; and the role of third parties in considering compliance.

8.2 The relationship between developing and developed states

The relationship between developing and developed states is perhaps one of the most salient elements in the development of international environmental law. It can be characterized in terms of both continuity and change.

On the one hand nature protection in developing states, in Africa in particular, continues to be of concern to developed states and NGOs based in developed states, such as WWF. On the other hand WWF's policy on CBNRM marks change in that it focuses on decision-making by and benefits for local populations (sections 2.3, 2.5). Similarly, the Nagoya Protocol requires the prior informed consent of and benefit sharing with indigenous and local communities when genetic resources or knowledge about these resources are accessed (section 4.5.6).

More generally, developing states in their implementation of MEAs continue to be dependent on developed states both directly and indirectly. The latter by way of the role of the World Bank, in particular. The World Bank in important ways coordinates the implementation of MEAs in developing states by way of its own financial resources, the GEF and GEF's Agencies, the PCF and the many funds that it or the GEF administer (section 5.5). As a result of its position the World Bank exercises considerable public powers in developing states.

The position of the World Bank is problematic for at least two reasons. First, it removes decision-making from the one-state-one-vote system, and in practice decision-making by consensus, which operates in MEAs, to the decision-making procedures of the Bank and the various funds it manages. These procedures involve decision-making by bodies of limited representation, weighted voting and may also involve private sector actors in decision-making. This situation raises issues of fairness in international environmental law and, as mentioned above, takes away from the promise of justice inherent in principles such as the principles of sustainable development, common but differentiated responsibilities and intra- and inter-generational equity. As a result, the relationship between developing and developed states remains one that is marked by political tension.

Second, it provides a single actor with a large amount of possibly universalizing power in deciding what sustainable development in developing states might entail. This approach runs the risk of treating developing states as a homogenous group. For example, in terms of how water resource management and supply should be organized, where in the past the World Bank focused on privatization of the sector, regardless of local context, at present, the World Bank's utilizes a more demand-driven and multi-stakeholder approach, which is more likely to enable local concerns to play a role in how water is managed and supplied.

Despite the above, the principle of common but differentiated responsibilities has brought about change in the position of developing states in international environmental law. As mentioned above, this principle has served to empower developing states in environmental negotiations by normalizing arguments related to their situation of under-development, the legacy of colonialism and the uneven distribution of wealth across the globe. Pertinent is the question whether, and if so how, the principle of common but differentiated responsibilities will be instrumental in translating emerging further socio-economic differentiation between states into international environmental law. The challenge faced in this context is perhaps best characterized as how we might move away from the developing-developed dichotomy to a perspective that focuses on how our social systems relate to the Earth's systems, including local ecosystems.

8.3   Institutional fragmentation

In terms of actors, the position of MEAs and international organizations probably marks the biggest change. At the beginning of the twentieth century these bodies did not play a role in international environmental law, for they did not exist. Today they play a prominent role in international environmental law. This role also comes with institutional fragmentation.

The solution to the institutional fragmentation of international environmental law according to some is the establishment of an international environmental organization. Such proposals are not new; ever since the establishment of UNEP was considered, during the preparations for the Stockholm Conference in the late 1960s/early 1970s, it has been suggested that an international environmental organization be established. Political interests made this impossible at the time. These interests were related to the competences of various existing international organizations, such as the IMO, IAEA and FAO, and the dominant position of developed states in some of these organizations at the time. The result was that UNEP was established as a programme of UNGA, and thus with a limited budget and limited powers (sections 2.3, 5.5). If established today, which seems highly unlikely from a political point of view, an international environmental organization might encompass some of the global MEAs. However, it seems unlikely that an international environmental organization would also encompass the work related to the protection and conservation of the environment carried out by international organizations such the IMO, the IAEA, the FAO and the World Bank. Political reasons may serve to explain this situation, but so does a normative argument related to the integration principle. For it is within these and other international organizations that international environmental law is being integrated into other policy areas such as shipping, the use of nuclear materials, agriculture and fisheries and the financing of development. In other words, within these international organizations the normative implications of the integration principle are being practised.

The above is not to say that further institutional linkages between the very many international bodies involved in international environmental law would not make sense. The joint secretariat established for the Basel, Stockholm and Rotterdam Conventions provides a promising example. Similar initiatives might make sense for conventions that focus on nature and biodiversity protection such as CITES and the Biodiversity, Bonn, Desertification and Ramsar Conventions or for the two global fisheries conventions, the Fish Stocks Agreement and the Compliance Agreement.

8.4 Emerging similarities between the roles of NGOs and private-sector actors

As participants in international negotiations, based on their position as observers, NGOs and private-sector actors have and continue to co-determine the content of international environmental law instruments adopted by states. This situation is comparable to the role that NGOs focused on nature conservation played in developing the early beginnings of international environmental law instruments (section 2.2).

The role of NGOs has also changed. Today they independently engage in normative development and in executive decision-making. Think of FSC and WWF (section 2.5). Conservation International, IUCN and WWF as GEF agencies, and before 2015 as beneficiaries of GEF funding, have strong links with the GEF (section 5.5). This new role might entail that these organizations are better classified as stakeholder organizations, for they no longer fit the picture of environmental lobby groups or of observers at meetings because they have a financial interest in the projects that are invested in by financial institutions. These NGO/stakeholder organizations, as private-sector actors, also seem to be answering the call for public-private partnerships, which emerged forcefully at the World Summit on Sustainable Development (section 2.3).

This new role of NGOs/stakeholder organizations, like the role of private sector actors, however remains under-conceptualized in terms of international environmental law (section 4.8). A question that arises in this context, for example, is how private sector actors accessing IFC/MIGA loans and NGOs/stakeholder organizations involved in the execution of GEF projects relate to the principles discussed in Chapter 4 or to the content of the MEA and related COP decisions that the loan or project seeks to implement. Additionally, how do the internal rules of NGO/stakeholder organizations, such as WWFs' CBNRM, relate to those of the GEF or other international bodies, such as the World Bank, whose projects they might be executing? These questions point to challenges that arise as new environmental governance arrangements emerge.

8.5   Linking the local and the global in regulatory approaches

Continuity and change also marks the regulatory approaches that have been developed in international environmental law over time. On the one hand, regulatory approaches for nature conservation developed in the early twentieth century continue to be important in contemporary environmental regimes. Relevant examples are the listing of species, protected areas and measures prohibiting or restricting trade in certain species. Similarly, approaches to reducing operational pollution that emerged during the late 1980s, such as BAT and BEP, as well as approaches to preventing accidental pollution continue to be relevant today.

On the other hand, new approaches have been introduced which focus on the regulation of trade in hazardous substances (section 3.5). These regimes employ prior informed consent procedures and use risk assessment as a means of regulation. As mentioned above, risk assessment procedure are expert and science-driven and as a means of regulation may pose challenges for states who cannot mobilize the required expertise. A similar problem manifests itself in the WTO where risk assessment plays an important role in determining whether, for example, SPS measures adopted by a state are compatible with WTO law (section 7.4.3). Risk assessment procedures tend to be internationalized and members of epistemic communities tend to be involved in their execution. As a result, the link to the local may be lost. While the Nagoya Protocol seeks to foster that link by way of the concept of benefit sharing, the regimes focused on international trade in hazardous substances to a lesser degree, and in some cases hardly at all, provide such a link. Think of the Rotterdam Convention (section 3.5.1). It has been suggested that risk assessment procedures should be more participatory, giving rise to the term "civic science" and implying that individuals and groups in society should have a say in whether they want to accept, for example, genetically modified organisms or hazardous chemicals in their environment. Such a proposal obviously challenges the very essence of risk assessment procedures.

8.6   The role of third parties in assessing state responsibility and compliance

Continuity and change also mark the manner in which international environmental law has dealt with issues of state responsibility and compliance. On the one hand, the use of inter-state judicial dispute settlement procedures continues to be the exception. However, when these procedures are used they may make a difference. The early *Trail Smelter* arbitration and the more recent *Pulp Mills* case decided by the ICJ, illustrate this point. *Trail Smelter* stands at the base of the mainstreaming of the no harm principle in international environmental law (sections 2.3, 4.5.1), and *Pulp Mills* is likely to be remembered for standing at the base of mainstreaming the principle of equitable and reasonable utilization in international watercourse law and possibly with regard to the use of transboundary resources more generally (section 4.5.2).

On the other hand, considerable change has been introduced in how compliance with international environmental law is dealt with. Instead of inter-state disputes in which state responsibility is assessed, various types of accountability mechanisms that assess compliance have been introduced (sections 6.3, 6.4). These mechanisms have changed the way we think about legally relevant relationships in international environmental law. We now accept that such relationships may involve, IDBs and individuals and groups in society as well as private-sector actors. Think of the FSC. Accountability mechanisms also provide a lesson: if we want compliance to be reviewed it is crucial to involve a third party or individuals in the process. This point is underscored by the compliance mechanisms of the Montreal Protocol and CITES, in which their respective secretariats play an important role; by the compliance mechanism of the Kyoto Protocol, in which expert review teams play an important role; as well as by the role that individuals and groups in society play in IDB grievance mechanisms and the Aarhus Convention compliance mechanism. Securing the role of third parties in accountability mechanisms will be challenging, as such mechanisms are being criticized for being too intrusive. The successor to the Kyoto Protocol will provide the opportunity for assessing whether the international community lives up to this challenge.

8.7   Final remarks

Continuity and change characterize the development of international environmental law, with both aspects presenting challenges for the future development of this body of law, including how it relates to other areas of international law. The suggestion that international environmental law might be integrated into the law of armed conflict via human rights law (section 7.3.2) is interesting in terms of change, for it might more generally offer a way of addressing the fragmented nature of international law and serve to implement the integration principle (section 4.7.1). Addressing fragmentation is a challenge that international environmental law shares with other areas of international law.

The biggest challenge facing international environmental law and law more in general is perhaps whether law manages to mediate the relationship between humans and their social systems, on the one hand, and ecological systems, on the other hand. The term "social-ecological system" captures this relationship, and the realization that we are living in the Anthropocene suggests that it is imperative that we address this relationship. International environmental law and law more generally, however, remain far removed from mediating this relationship. Perhaps giving local contexts a more prominent place within international environmental law and rethinking the relationships between various levels of governance in terms of law offer part of the answer. The assessment of investor-state arbitrations and their relationship to local remedies provides an example of how we might re-think governance arrangements (section 7.5). Why this focus on the local? Because it is in local contexts that the hard work of protecting and conserving the environment needs to be done and that the consequences of environmental degradation are experienced.

Table of cases

Short title	Full title and citation
ACCC/C/2008/24, Spain	ACCC, Findings and recommendations with regard to communication ACCC/C/2008/24 concerning compliance by Spain, 15–18 December 2009.
ACCC/C/2008/32 Part I, European Union	ACCC, Findings and recommendations with regard to communication ACCC/C/2008/32 (Part I) concerning compliance by the European Union, 14 April 2011.
ACCC/C/2008/33, United Kingdom	ACCC, Findings and recommendations with regard to communication ACCC/C/2008/33 concerning compliance by the United Kingdom of Great Britain and Northern Ireland, 24 September 2010.
ACCC/C/2009/41, Slovakia	ACCC, Findings and recommendations with regard to communication ACCC/C/2009/41 concerning compliance by Slovakia, 17 December 2010.
ACCC/C/2010/54, European Union	ACCC, Findings and recommendations with regard to communication ACCC/C/2010/54 concerning compliance by the European Union, 29 June 2012.
Arctic Sunrise case	ITLOS, *The Arctic Sunrise Case* (Kingdom of the Netherlands v. Russian Federation), Provisional Measures, Case No. 22, 22 November 2013.
	Arctic Sunrise Arbitration (Kingdom of the Netherlands v. Russian Federation), (An Arbitral Tribunal Constituted under Annex VII to the 1982 United Nations Convention on the Law of the Sea), Award on the Merits, PCA 2014-02, 14 August 2015.
Brazil–Retreaded Tyres	WTO AB, *Brazil – Measures Affecting Imports of Retreaded Tyres (Brazil – Retreaded Tyres)*, AB-2007-4 WT/DS332/AB/R (Report of the Appellate Body), 3 December 2007.

Short title	Full title and citation
Canada–Renewable Energy	WTO AB, *Canada – Certain Measures Affecting the Renewable Energy Generation Sector (Canada – Renewable Energy)*, AB-2013-1, WT/DS412/AB/R (Report of the Appellate Body), 6 May 2013.
Chevron/Texaco (Lago Agrio) cases	Second International Water Tribunal, *Petroleum in the Ecuadorian Amazon Water Pollution Due to Petroleum Exploitation* (Corporation of Legal-ecological Investigation and Defense of Life (CORDAVI) v. Petroecuador, Texaco Petroleum Company & City Investigating Company), Second International Water Tribunal, *Pollution*, Vol. 7 of the Case Books, International Books, 1994, p. 63.
	International Rights of Nature Tribunal Lima, *Ecuadorian Amazon v. Chevron-Texaco*, Final Verdict, 5–6 December 2014.
	Also see *Kichwa Indigenous People of Sarayaku v. Ecuador.*
	For an overview of these and the many other cases involved in the Chevron/Texaco litigation see "The Chevron-Ecuador Dispute: A Paradigm of Complexity" with contributions by Dan Bodansky, Judith Kimerling, Lucinda Low, Ralph G. Steinhardt and Christopher Whytock, in *American Society of International Law. Proceedings of the Annual Meeting*, 2012, pp. 415–28.
Commission v. France	ECJ, *Commission v. France*, Case C-182/89, [1990] ECR I-4337, 29 November 1990.
Concerning Land Reclamation by Singapore in and around the Straits of Johor	ITLOS, *Case concerning Land Reclamation by Singapore in and around the Straits of Johor* (Malaysia v. Singapore), Provisional Measures, Case No. 12, 8 October 2003.
	Concerning Land Reclamation by Singapore in and around the Straits of Johor (Malaysia v. Singapore), Award on Agreed Terms, PCA, 1 September 2005.
Corfu Channel case	ICJ, *The Corfu Channel Case*, Judgement, ICJ Reports 1949, p. 4, 9 April 1949.

Short title	Full title and citation
EC–Asbestos	WTO AB, *European Communities – Measures Affecting Asbestos and Asbestos-Containing Products (European Communities – Asbestos)*, AB-2000-11, WT/DS135/AB/R (Report of the Appellate Body), 12 March 2001.
EC–Hormones	WTO AB, *European Communities – Measures Concerning Meat and Meat Products (Hormones)*, AB-1997-4, WT/DS26/AB/R WT/DS48/AB/R (Report of the Appellate Body), 16 January 1998.
Fadeyeva v. Russia	ECtHR, *Fadeyeva v. Russia*, (Chamber), Application No. 55723/00, 9 June 2005.
Gabčíkovo-Nagymaros	ICJ, *Gabčíkovo-Nagymaros Project* (Hungary v. Slovakia), Judgment, ICJ Reports 1997, p. 7, 25 September 1997.
Hatton v. UK	ECtHR, *Hatton and Others v. United Kingdom*, (Grand Chamber), Application No. 36022/97, 8 July 2003.
India NTPC Power Generation Project	WBIP, *India NTPC Power Generation Project,* Case 10, 24 July 1997.
Iron Rhine arbitration	*Regarding the Iron Rhine ("IJzeren Rijn") Railway (The Kingdom of Belgium and the Kingdom of the Netherlands)*, Reports of International Arbitral Awards, Vol. XXVII, p. 35, 24 May 2005.
Japan–Measures Affecting the Importation of Apples	WTO AB, *Japan – Measures Affecting the Importation of Apples*, AB-2003-4, WT/DS245/AB/R (Report of the Appellate Body), 26 November 2003.
Kenya Natural Resource Management Project	WBIP, *Kenya Natural Resource Management Project,* Case 84, 22 May 2014.
Kichwa Indigenous People of Sarayaku v. Ecuador	IACtHR, *Case of Kichwa Indigenous People of Sarayaku v. Ecuador*, Merits and Reparations, Series C No. 245, 27 June 2012.
Lac Lanoux arbitration	*Lac Lanoux Arbitration* (France v. Spain), Reports of International Arbitral Awards, Volume XII, p. 281, 16 November 1957.
López Ostra v. Spain	ECtHR, *López Ostra v. Spain*, (Chamber), Application No. 16798/90, 9 December 1994.

Short title	Full title and citation
Maya Indigenous Community of the Toledo District v. Belize	IAComHR, *Maya Indigenous Communities of the Toledo District v. Belize*, Case 12.053, Report No. 40/04, 12 October 2004.
Metalclad v. Mexico	*Metalclad Corporation v. the United Mexican States*, NAFTA, ICSID Case No. ARB (AF)/97/1, 30 August 2000.
Methanex v. US	*Methanex Corporation v. United States of America*, Final Award on Jurisdiction and Merits, NAFTA, UNCITRAL, 44 ILM 1345 (2005), 3 August 2005.
Minors Oposa	Supreme Court of the Philippines, *Minors Oposa v. Secretary of the Department of Environmental and Natural Resources*, 33 ILM 173 (1994), 30 July 1993.
MOX Plant case	ITLOS, *The MOX Plant Case* (Ireland v. United Kingdom), Provisional Measures, Case No. 10, 3 December 2001.
	The MOX Plant Case (Ireland v. United Kingdom), (Arbitral Tribunal Constituted Pursuant to Article 287, and Article 1 of Annex VII, of the United Nations Convention on the Law of the Sea for the Dispute Concerning the MOX Plant, International Movements of Radioactive Materials, and the Protection of the Marine Environment of the Irish Sea), Termination of Procedures, Order No. 6, 6 June 2008.
Nuclear Weapons	ICJ, *Legality of the Threat or Use of Nuclear Weapons*, Advisory Opinion, ICJ Reports 1996, p. 226, 8 July 1996.
Ogoniland Case	ACHPR, *The Social and Economic Rights Action Center and the Center for Economic and Social Rights v. Nigeria*, Comm. No. 155/96 (2001), 27 October 2001.
Öneryildiz v. Turkey	ECtHR, *Öneryildiz v. Turkey*, (Grand Chamber), Application No. 48939/99, 30 November 2004.
Pacific or Bering Sea Fur Seal arbitration	*Award between the United States and the United Kingdom relating to the rights of jurisdiction of United States in the Bering Sea and the preservation of fur seals*, Report of International Arbitral Awards, Vol. XXVIII, p. 263, 15 August 1893.

Short title	Full title and citation
Tecmed v. Mexico	*Award in the matter of the arbitration between Technicas Medioambientales Techmed S.A. and The United Mexican States*, NAFTA, ICSID, Case No. ARB (AF)/00/2, 29 May 2003.
Trail Smelter arbitration	*Award in the Trail Smelter Arbitration between United States and Canada*, 11 March 1941, Reports of International Arbitral Awards, Volume III, p. 1938.
US–Continued Suspension	WTO AB, *United States – Continued Suspension of Obligations in the EC – Hormones Dispute*, AB-2008-5, WT/DS320/AB/R (Report of the Appellate Body), 16 October 2008.
US–Gasoline	WTO AB, *United States – Standards for Reformulated and Conventional Gasoline*, AB-1996-1, WT/DS2/AB/R (Report of the Appellate Body), 29 April 1996.
US–Shrimp	WTO AB, *United States – Import Prohibition of Certain Shrimp and Shrimp Products*, AB-1998-4, WT/DS58/AB/R (Report of the Appellate Body), 12 October 1998.
US–Tuna II	WTO AB, *United States – Measures Concerning the Importation, Marketing and Sale of Tuna and Tuna Products*, AB-2012-2, WT/DS381/AB/R (Report of the Appellate Body), 16 May 2012.
Veracel Brazil	Assessment Report: ASI-REP-54-SGS QUALIFOR – 2011 – Brazil (Veracel), FSC, 18 April 2011 to 20 April 2011, available at http://asi.df-kunde.de/resources/document-library?did=80.
Whaling in the Antarctic	ICJ, *Whaling in the Antarctic* (Australia v. Japan: New Zealand intervening), Judgement, ICJ Reports 2014, p. 226, 31 March 2014.

Table of instruments

Short title	Year of adoption and full title	Entry into force, for treaties and MOUs
1900 Convention	1900 London Convention for the Preservation of Wild Animals, Birds and Fish in Africa	No longer in force
1902 Convention	1902 Paris Convention to Protect Birds Useful to Agriculture	No longer in force
1933 Convention	1933 London Convention Relative to the Preservation of Fauna and Flora in their Natural State	No longer in force
Aarhus Convention	1998 Aarhus Convention on Access to Information, Public Participation in Decision-making and Access to Justice in Environmental Matters, adopted within the UNECE	30 October 2001
Additional Protocol I	1977 Protocol Additional to the Geneva Conventions of 12 August 1949, and relating to the Protection of Victims of International Armed Conflicts	7 December 1978
Additional Protocol to the American Convention	1988 Additional Protocol to the American Convention on Human Rights	16 November 1999
African–Eurasian Waterbirds Agreement	1996 Agreement on the Conservation of African–Eurasian Migratory Waterbirds	1 November 1999
African Nature Conservation Convention	1968 African Convention on the Conservation of Nature and Natural Resource	16 June 1969

Short title	Year of adoption and full title	Entry into force, for treaties and MOUs
Agreement on Cetaceans of the Black Sea, Mediterranean Sea and Contiguous Atlantic Area	1996 Agreement on the Conservation of Cetaceans of the Black Sea, Mediterranean Sea and Contiguous Atlantic Area	1 May 2001
Agreement on Marine Mammals in the North Atlantic	1992 Agreement on Cooperation in Research, Conservation and Management of Marine Mammals in the North Atlantic	10 September 1994
Agreement on Small Cetaceans of the Baltic and North Seas	1991 Agreement on the Conservation of Small Cetaceans of the Baltic and North Seas	29 March 1994
	2008 Amendment to include the North East Atlantic and Irish Seas	3 February 2008
Agreement on the Limpopo Commission	2003 Agreement on the Establishment of the Limpopo Watercourse Commission	5 November 2011
Agreement on the Mekong River	1995 Agreement on Cooperation for the Sustainable Development of the Mekong River Basin	5 April 1995
AIDCP	1998 Agreement on the International Dolphin Conservation Programme	15 February 1999
Antarctic Environmental Protocol	1991 Protocol on Environmental Protection to the Antarctic Treaty	14 January 1998
Antarctic Treaty	1959 Antarctic Treaty	23 June 1961
Anti-fouling Convention	2001 International Convention on the Control of Harmful Anti-fouling Systems on Ships	17 September 2008
Anti-Personnel Mines Convention	1997 Convention on the Prohibition of the Use, Stockpiling, Production and Transfer of Anti-Personnel Mines and on Their Destruction	1 March 1999

Short title	Year of adoption and full title	Entry into force, for treaties and MOUs
Arab Charter of Human Rights	2004 Arab Charter of Human Rights	16 March 2008
Articles on State Responsibility	2007 Articles on the Responsibility of States for Internationally Wrongful Acts, adopted by the UN General Assembly in 2007	
ASEAN Human Rights Declaration	2012 Human Rights Declaration adopted by the Association of Southeast Asian Nations	
Assistance Convention	1986 Convention on Assistance in the Case of a Nuclear Accident or Radiological Emergency	27 February 1987
Ballast Water Convention	2004 International Convention for the Control and Management of Ships Ballast Water & Sediments	Not in force
Bamako Convention	1991 Convention on the Ban of the Import into Africa and the Control of Transboundary Movement and Management of Hazardous Wastes within Africa	22 April 1998
Banjul Charter	1981 African Charter on Human and Peoples Rights	21 October 1986
Basel Convention	1989 Basel Convention on the Control of Transboundary Movement of Hazardous Wastes and their Disposal	5 May 1992
Biodiversity Convention	1992 Convention on the Conservation of Biological Diversity	29 December 1993
Biodiversity and Wilderness Conservation Convention	1992 Convention for the Conservation of the Biodiversity and the Protection of Wilderness Areas in Central America	20 December 1994
Biological Weapons Convention	1972 Convention on the Prohibition of the Development, Production and Stockpiling of Bacteriological (Biological) Weapons and Toxic Weapons and their Destruction	26 March 1975

Short title	Year of adoption and full title	Entry into force, for treaties and MOUs
Bonn Agreement	1969 Agreement for Cooperation in Dealing with Pollution of the North Sea by Oil	9 August 1969
	1983 Amendment to include other harmful substances	1 September 1989
Bonn Convention	1979 Convention on the Conservation of Migratory Species of Wild Animals	1 November 1983
Boundary Waters Treaty	1909 Treaty Relating to Boundary Waters and Questions Arising Between the United States and Canada	5 May 1910
Brussels Supplementary Convention	1963 Convention Supplementary to the 1960 Paris Convention on Third Party Liability in the Field of Nuclear Energy	4 December 1974
Cartagena Protocol	2000 Cartagena Protocol on Biosafety to the Convention on Biological Diversity	11 September 2003
CITES	1973 Convention on International Trade in Endangered Species of Wild Fauna and Flora	1 July 1975
Civil Liability Convention	1969 Convention on Civil Liability for Oil Pollution Damage	19 June 1975
COLREG	1972 Convention for the International Regulation for the Prevention of Collisions at Sea	15 July 1977
Compliance Agreement	1993 FAO Agreement to Promote Compliance with International Conservation and Management Measures by Fishing Vessels on the High Seas	24 April 2003
Convention on Certain Conventional Weapons	1980 Convention on Prohibitions or Restrictions on the Use of Certain Conventional Weapons which may be Deemed to be Excessively Injurious or to Have Indiscriminate Effects	2 December 1983

Short title	Year of adoption and full title	Entry into force, for treaties and MOUs
Convention on Cluster Munitions	2008 Convention on Cluster Munitions	1 August 2010
Convention on the Protection of Nuclear Material	1980 Convention on the Physical Protection of Nuclear Material	7 February 1987
Convention on the Rights of the Child	1989 Convention on the Rights of the Child	2 September 1990
Desertification Convention	1994 Convention to Combat Desertification in those Countries Experiencing Serious Drought and /or Desertification, particularly in Africa	16 December 1996
Doha Amendment to the Kyoto Protocol	2012 Doha Amendment to the Kyoto Protocol of the UNFCCC	Not in force
ENMOD Convention	1977 Convention on the Prohibition of Military or Any Hostile Use of Environmental Modification Techniques	5 October 1978
Espoo Convention	1991 Espoo Convention on Environmental Impact Assessment in a Transboundary Context, adopted within the UNECE	10 September 1997
Fish Stocks Agreement	1995 Agreement for the Implementation of the Provisions of the United Nations Convention on the Law of the Sea of 10 December 1982 relating to the Conservation and Management of Straddling Fish Stocks and Highly Migratory Fish Stocks	11 December 2001
Fund Convention	1971 Convention on the Establishment of an International Fund for Compensation for Oil Pollution Damage	16 October 1978
Fur Seals Convention	1911 Convention for the Preservation and Protection of the Fur Seals	No longer in force

Short title	Year of adoption and full title	Entry into force, for treaties and MOUs
GATT	1994 General Agreement on Tariffs and Trade	1 January 1995
Great Lakes Agreement	1972 Great Lakes Water Quality Agreement	15 April 1972
Hague Convention for Protection of Cultural Property	1954 Hague Convention for the Protection of Cultural Property in the Event of Armed Conflict	7 August 1956
Hamilton Declaration on the Sargasso Sea	2014 Hamilton Declaration on Collaboration of the Conservation of the Sargasso Sea	
Helsinki Convention	1992 Convention on the Protection of the Marine Environment of the Baltic Sea Area	17 January 2000
Helsinki Water Convention	1992 Convention on the Protection and Use of Transboundary Watercourses and International Lakes, adopted within the UNECE	6 October 1996
HNS Convention	1996 Convention on Liability and Compensation for Damage in Connection with the Carriage of Hazardous and Noxious Substances by Sea	Not in force
HNS Protocol	2010 Protocol to the International Convention on Liability and Compensation for Damage in Connection with the Carriage of Hazardous and Noxious Substances by Sea, 1996	Not in force
Hong Kong Convention	2009 Hong Kong International Convention for the Safe and Environmentally Sound Recycling of Ships	Not in force
ICC Statute	1998 Statute of the International Criminal Court	1 July 2001
ICESCR	1966 International Covenant on Economic, Social and Cultural Rights	3 January 1976

Short title	Year of adoption and full title	Entry into force, for treaties and MOUs
ILA Declaration	2002 New Delhi Declaration of Principles of International Law Relating to Sustainable Development	
ILC Articles on the Prevention of Transboundary Harm	2001 Articles on the Prevention of Transboundary Harm from Hazardous Activities	
ILO Convention 169	1989 ILO Convention 169 on Indigenous and Tribal Peoples in Independent Countries	5 September 1991
Industrial Accidents Convention	1992 Convention on the Transboundary Effects of Industrial Accidents, adopted within the UNECE	19 April 2000
International Guidelines on High Seas Deep-sea Fisheries	2008 FAO International Guidelines for the Management of Deep-sea Fisheries in the High Seas	
International Whaling Convention	1946 International Convention for the Regulation of Whaling	10 November 1948
Intervention Convention	1969 Convention Relating to Intervention on the High Seas in Cases of Oil Pollution Casualties	6 May 1975
IUCN Draft Covenant	1995 IUCN Draft International Covenant on Environment and Development	
Johannesburg Declaration	2002 Johannesburg Declaration on Sustainable Development	
Joint Convention on Spent Fuel and Radioactive Waste	1997 Joint Convention on the Safety of Spent Fuel Management and on the Safety of Radioactive Waste Management	8 June 2001

Short title	Year of adoption and full title	Entry into force, for treaties and MOUs
Joint Protocol	1988 Joint Protocol Relating to the Application of the 1963 Vienna Convention on Civil Liability for Nuclear Damage and the1960 Paris Convention on Third Party Liability in the Field of Nuclear Energy	27 April 1992
Kyoto Protocol	1997 Kyoto Protocol to the United Nations Framework Convention on Climate Change	16 February 2005
London Convention	1972 London Convention on the Prevention of Marine Pollution by Dumping of Wastes and Other Matter	30 August 1972
LOS Convention	1982 United Nations Convention on the Law of the Sea	16 November 1994
LRTAP Convention	1979 Convention on Long-range Transboundary Air Pollution, adopted within the UNECE	16 March 1983
Maritime Labour Convention	2006 Maritime Labour Convention	20 August 2013
MARPOL Convention	73/78 International Convention for the Prevention of Marine Pollution from Ships	2 October 1983
Minamata Convention	2013 Minamata Convention on Mercury	Not in force
Montreal Protocol	1987 Montreal Protocol to the Vienna Convention on the Protection of the Ozone Layer	1 January 1989
MOU on High Andean Flamingos	2008 Memorandum of Understanding on the Conservation of High Andean Flamingos and their Habitats	8 December 2008
MOU on the Slender-billed Curlew	1994 Memorandum of Understanding on the Conservation Measures for the Slender-billed Curlew	10 September 1994

Short title	Year of adoption and full title	Entry into force, for treaties and MOUs
MOU on West African Populations of the African Elephant	2005 Memorandum of Understanding concerning Conservation Measures for the West African Populations of the African Elephant	22 November 2005
NAFTA	1992 North American Free Trade Agreement	1 January 1994
Nagoya Protocol	2010 Nagoya Protocol on Access to Genetic Resources and the Fair and Equitable Sharing of Benefits from their Utilization	12 October 2014
Non-Proliferation Treaty	1968 Treaty on the Non-Proliferation of Nuclear Weapons	5 March 1970
Notification Convention	1986 Convention on Early Notification of a Nuclear Accident	27 October 1986
OILPOL Convention	1954 International Convention for the Prevention of Pollution of the Sea by Oil	26 July 1958
OPRC Convention	1990 International Convention on Oil Pollution Preparedness, Response and Co-operation	3 May 1995
OPRC-HNS Protocol	2000 Protocol on Preparedness, Response and Co-operation to Pollution Incidents by Hazardous and Noxious Substances	14 June 2007
OSPAR Convention	1992 Convention for the Protection of the Marine Environment of the North-East Atlantic	25 March 1998
Paris Convention	1974 Convention for the Prevention of Marine Pollution from Land-based Sources	6 May 1978
Paris Convention on Third Party Liability in the Field of Nuclear Energy	1960 Paris Convention on Third Party Liability in the Field of Nuclear Energy	1 April 1968

Short title	Year of adoption and full title	Entry into force, for treaties and MOUs
Paris MOU on Port State Control	1982 Paris Memorandum of Understanding on Port State Control	Operational 1 July 1982
Polar Bear Agreement	1973 International Agreement on the Conservation of Polar Bears	26 May 1976
POPs Protocol to the LRTAP Convention	Protocol to the 1979 Convention on Long-range Transboundary Air Pollution on Persistent Organic Pollutants	23 October 2003
Principles on Business and Human Rights	2011 Guiding Principles on Business and Human Rights: Implementing the United Nations "Protect, Respect and Remedy" Framework	
Protocol for Sustainable Development of Lake Victoria Basin	2003 Protocol for Sustainable Development of Lake Victoria Basin to the Treaty for the Establishment of the East African Community	1 December 2004
Protocol to Amend the Vienna Convention on Civil Liability for Nuclear Damage	1997 Protocol to Amend the 1963 Vienna Convention on Civil Liability for Nuclear Damage	4 October 2003
Protocol to the Intervention Convention	1973 Protocol Relating to Intervention on the High Seas in Cases of Pollution by Substances other than Oil	30 March 1983
Protocol to the London Convention	1996 Protocol to the Convention on the Prevention of Marine Pollution by Dumping of Wastes and Other Matter	27 March 2006
PRTR Protocol	2003 Protocol on Pollutant Release and Transfer Registers to the Convention on Access to Information, Public Participation in Decision-making and Access to Justice in Environmental Matters, adopted within the UNECE	9 October 2009

Short title	Year of adoption and full title	Entry into force, for treaties and MOUs
Ramsar Convention	1971 Ramsar Convention on Wetlands of International Importance	21 December 1975
Revised African Nature Conservation Convention	2003 Revised African Convention on the Conservation of Nature and Natural Resources	Not in force
Rhine Convention	1999 Convention on the Protection on the Rhine	1 January 2003
Rio Declaration	1992 Rio Declaration on Environment and Development	
River Uruguay Statute	1975 Statute for the River Uruguay	18 September 1976
Rotterdam Convention	1998 Rotterdam Convention on the Prior Informed Consent Procedure for Certain Hazardous Chemicals and Pesticides in International Trade	24 February 2004
SADC Water Protocol	2000 Revised Protocol on Shared Watercourses in Southern African Development Community	22 September 2003
Safety Convention	1994 Nuclear Safety Convention	24 October 1996
Salvage Convention	1989 International Convention on Salvage	14 July 1996
SCM Agreement	1994 Agreement on Subsidies and Countervailing Measures	1 January 1995
SEA Protocol	2003 Protocol on Strategic Environmental Assessment to the Espoo Convention, adopted within the UNECE	11 July 2010
SOLAS Convention	1974 Convention on the Safety of Life at Sea	25 May 1980
SPS Agreement	1994 Agreement on Sanitary and Phytosanitary Measures	1 January 1995

Short title	Year of adoption and full title	Entry into force, for treaties and MOUs
Statement on Forests	1992 Non-Legally Binding Authoritative Statement of Principles for a Global Consensus on the Management, Conservation and Sustainable Development of All Types of Forests	
STCW Convention	1978 Convention on Standards of Training, Certification and Watchkeeping for Seafarers	28 April 1984
Stockholm Convention	2001 Stockholm Convention on Persistent Organic Pollutants	17 May 2004
Stockholm Declaration	1972 Stockholm Declaration on the Human Environment	
Supplementary Convention	1997 Convention on Supplementary Compensation for Nuclear Damage	Not in force
Supplementary Convention to TOVALOP	1971 Contract Regarding an Interim Supplement to Tanker Liability for Oil Pollution	No longer in force
TBT Agreement	1994 Agreement on Technical Barriers to Trade	1 January 1995
"The Future We Want"	2012 "The Future We Want", final document adopted at Rio +20	
TOVALOP	1966 Tanker Owners Voluntary Agreement concerning Liability for Oil Pollution	No longer in force
Treaty on Salmon Fishing in the Rhine	1885 Treaty Concerning the Regulation of Salmon Fishery in the Rhine River Basin	No longer in force
Treaty on the Functioning of the European Union	2007 Treaty on the Functioning of the European Union	1 December 2009
TRIMs Agreement	1994 Agreement on Trade-Related Investment Measures	1 January 1995
UNFCCC	1992 United Nations Framework Convention on Climate Change	21 March 1994

Short title	Year of adoption and full title	Entry into force, for treaties and MOUs
United Nations Charter	1945 Charter of the United Nations	24 October 1945
Vienna Convention on Civil Liability for Nuclear Damage	1963 Vienna Convention on Civil Liability for Nuclear Damage	12 November 1977
Vienna Convention on the Ozone Layer	1985 Vienna Convention on the Protection of the Ozone Layer	22 September 1988
Wadden Sea Seals Agreement	1990 Agreement on the Conservation of Seals in the Wadden Sea	16 October 1991
Watercourses Convention	1997 Convention on the Law of the Non-Navigable Uses of International Watercourses	17 August 2014
WCED Principles	1987 Proposed Legal Principles for Environmental Protection and Sustainable Development developed by the WCED Experts Group on Environmental Law	
Western Hemisphere Convention	1940 Convention on Nature Protection and Wild Life Preservation in the Western Hemisphere	1 May 1942
World Charter for Nature	1982 World Charter for Nature adopted by UNGA (UNGA Res. 37/7(1982))	
World Heritage Convention	1972 Convention Concerning the Protection of the World Cultural and Natural Heritage	17 December 1975
WTO Agreement	1994 Agreement Establishing the World Trade Organization	1 January 1995

Index